**SOMEDAY
IT'LL ALL BE YOURS
. . . OR WILL IT?**

SOMEDAY
IT'LL ALL BE YOURS
... OR WILL IT?

Donald J. Jonovic, Ph.D.

JAMIESON PRESS
Cleveland

Published by JAMIESON PRESS
A Subsidiary of BUSINESS SUCCESSION RESOURCE CENTER, INC.
P.O. Box 909, Cleveland, Ohio 44120

Library of Congress Cataloging in Publication Data

Jonovic, Donald J., 1943-
  Someday it'll all be yours . . . or will it?

  Includes index.
  1. Family corporations — Management. I. Title.
HD62.25.J663 1984   658'.045   83-26823
ISBN 0-915607-00-X

First Printing: January 1984

Second Printing: July 1984

Third Printing: February 1985

Printed in the United States of America

This one's for Pamela, too . . .
For love, understanding,
interest, help —
and, above all,
faith.

TABLE OF CONTENTS

SECTION III — THE PROCESS

ACKNOWLEDGEMENTS

The thoughts and ideas in this book grew and evolved over a decade of experience. During that time, I had the great fortune of working with many hundreds of people — business owners, their successors, their spouses and families, their suppliers, advisers, directors, and employees. Each of these people, in varying measure, has contributed to this book. Although I can't acknowledge them individually, if they read what is written here, they'll know who they are.

I ask each of them to accept my gratitude.

Special appreciation is owed to Dr. John L. Ward of Loyola University. During the many projects on which we collaborated, his unique insights had significant effects on my own thought. His positive influence is evident at many points in this book.

To my friend and colleague, George Steinbrenner, who has been so generous with his time reading and critiquing this and other writings, thanks.

And, finally, I would like to acknowledge the superb work that my wife, Pamela, did in editing the manuscript for publication. No editor has ever been tougher, more thorough, or less compromising on issues of content, clarity and accuracy. Her many dedicated hours could never fully be repaid.

PREFACE

Business ownership is one of our last frontiers. It beckons irresistibly to our rugged individuals, compulsive pioneers, and incurable heroes.

There's a certain romance, too, in owning one's business. There are prospects of wealth, control over one's destiny, and even the chance to work closely with people one loves and (more importantly) trusts.

For many fortunate family companies this is as true in practice as it is in theory — but it's not true for all. In fact, for the majority of successful family businesses, this great part of the American Dream remains as frustratingly elusive as a balanced national budget.

The prospect of owning a family business is a promised Utopia, but like most such dreams, the family business has a weakness that only becomes apparent when real people try to live it.

And what is this weakness?

The family. The very source of the company's greatest strength is also its weakest link.

Maybe this sounds like a contradiction, but it's a fact that many people who are *in* family companies see their families as obstacles, not assets. They're compelled by this perception into a continuing search for ways to separate family concerns from business problems, a desire that seems particularly common and strong among the second or inheriting generation.

Instead of reveling in the advantages of family ownership, many people who share businesses want to divorce family life from business life. In fact, many of these misguided clans have *policies* that business will *not* be discussed at family gatherings. Others, who don't have such policies, sometimes wish they did as another family Thanksgiving rolls around and the usual business "discussion" heats up over yet another cooling, uneaten turkey.

This all too common "divorce-wish" is the result of an epidemic carelessness among families in business. They fail to treat their families as the assets they really are.

EMOTIONAL SEASICKNESS

These "divorce prone" people aren't antisocial deviants. They're normal, nice people suffering from emotional confusion and disappointment. In spite of their financial success, and despite the fact that they've worked together for years, they find themselves aching to back away from a collaboration that was once among the most attractive reasons for working in the family business.

Business ownership can be like sailing in rough weather. The wind and the speed are exhilarating, but only if you're in control. With the family involved intimately in the business, the deck can get crowded with a sometimes unruly mob. It's bad enough when the crew isn't organized to work together, but it can get downright dangerous when people start fighting over control of the helm.

Small wonder everybody starts dreaming about solitude and peace.

Families in business travel, together, out in some pretty rough weather, day after day, season after season. It's tough to be stoic — let alone enthusiastic — when your own crew seems determined to turn you broadside to the waves. For those companies that have the proper discipline and organization, the journey can be an enticing, if risky, challenge, but for those who are poorly organized — as far too many are — the experience can be hell.

You'd think success with the business would make all this easier, but you'd be wrong. Success brings as many problems — to everybody in the family — as it solves. As time goes by, the people who need each other the most find it harder and harder to get along.

HOW SUCCESS WEARS ON DAD

For the founder (usually Dad, but males have no monopoly on entrepreneurship), business ownership is tough. It's also risky — and the uncertainties never really disappear, no matter how successful he becomes.

Business owners — even the successful ones — wake up unemployed every morning of their working lives. They teeter precariously from crisis to crisis, far above the relative security of a real job. *There are no safety nets,* and all success tends to do is raise their personal high wires further off the ground.

This is why successful business owners are so crusty. It's living with this uncertainty that underlies their uncompromising tenacity, pride, and drive. They know what it's like to lie awake in three a.m. "blink" sessions, staring at the all-too-familiar crack in the bedroom ceiling, wondering how they'll get through the coming day. The immediate problems may vary, but the underlying anxiety is the same.

The experience teaches them one thing for sure — there's only one person who can get them across their tightrope.

Who, you ask?

Hizzoner, of course: The Boss.

Each business owner "learns" during the early years that there's nobody he can depend on but himself. So he's tough. He's resourceful. And he's alone.

No question, The Boss of a successful family company has a lot going for him. He's a noticebly self-contained breed — and proud of it. But that also means he cuts himself off from the rest of the family, keeping an emotional distance that contradicts one of the major reasons he started his company in the first place.

Listen for a minute to one of his "blink" sessions:

"I'm really tired. Got to start taking it easier. But who's going to run this place? I don't think the kids can handle it. What would I do with myself — and where would I get the cash to do it? Why does my son's wife bug me so much . . ."

In spite of his power, worries flap around him in the dark, in ever-expanding circles. How will the business survive, he wonders, if the successors can't handle the job? And, even if they're competent, what good will it do if they can't get along?

What happens to a man who's worked all his life if he suddenly stops?

How does he secure his future if most of his net worth is tied up in the company? How can he get his money out, and if he can't, how can he trust his future to his children (whom he understands all too well) and their spouses (whom he's never understood at all)?

So much for sharing success with people he knows, trusts, and loves.

THE OTHERS IN THE BOAT

The Boss suffers all this in silence, of course, (recall how tough he is), but his isn't the only suffering. Dad's stiff (albeit quivering) upper lip, unknown to him, is being imitated in other dark bedrooms around town by other members of his family.

They, too, lie awake at three a.m. They wonder why Dad is so stubborn and secretive. They wonder why he doesn't trust them and why the business isn't the fun it used to be, or why their marriages are suddenly so explosive. Why, they wonder, is it harder and harder to get up in the morning? Why do the slightest disagreements become major blowouts? And why isn't the family close anymore?

Year after year, members of families in business tend to draw further apart. They watch in confusion as the primary blessing of business ownership seems to slip away into a fog of frustration and disagreement.

This is a side effect of family business success felt only by the insiders. What the outside world sees is "undeserved" wealth and "unwarranted" privilege, but, inside, the participants are hardly enjoying all of these so-called benefits. Instead, they continuously chew on indigestible problems. They worry them like a cat with a balled spider. They carry these problems home. They carry them to work. They carry them everywhere they go — and they each carry them alone.

How, they ask themselves, did nice people like us get into a situation like this?

Far too many successful family businesses suffer this way — isolated, inbred islands of discontent and confusion. It needn't happen, but as long as it does, days, months, and years will be wasted while the strength of the business slowly ebbs away.

THE FAMILY IS A MAJOR ASSET

For a family business to maintain success from generation to generation, the existence of the family has to be accepted, worked with, and used to advantage. Family is an asset, no less than the more tangible assets listed on the balance sheet, and it must be treated as such.

Why is it that family-owned distributorships succeed where "company stores" fail? Why is it that customers prefer working with family businesses? Why is it that most of our innovation, and a majority of our new jobs, are generated by private companies? It's because nobody pours as much energy, commitment, sweat, and funds into a business as do the owners of that business.

That's the asset side. But assets are only half of the balance sheet. As counterweights on the other side are equivalents either in equity or liability, and the objective of this book is to help eliminate the family liabilities that drain the company's health, and, at the same time, to increase that unique "equity" called mutual benefit.

As you might imagine, that's not a goal easily reached. But there are ways. There *are* ways we can learn to talk to each other without explosions. There *are* ways to recognize the difference between disagreements about facts and disagreements about values — and to react reasonably to each. There *are* ways to get along with daughters- and sons-in-law. There *are* ways to qualify and measure successors, to organize for growth, to get quality help and advice, and to plan estates and retirement.

In a sense, this is a book about divorce — the pain that leads up to it, the wasteful results of it, and the people it hurts. But I prefer to look at it as a book about reconciliation, cooperation, and commitment. I believe that a successful family business provides one of the most exciting economic opportunities one can have in our society, and I know from experience that it is, in fact, possible to benefit from that opportunity.

The solution is simple in concept. What's needed is a thorough and practical succession plan. But the challenge to put together a successful plan is one that's tough for any of us to meet. I won't pretend to have all the answers. Anyone who does is outright insensitive or a downright fraud. But thousands of family companies have done the job right, and from them we can learn some of the approaches and techniques that seem to work.

This book is, in essence, a report on the state of the art in management transition among successful family companies.

COMPONENTS OF A SUCCESSION PLAN

To give you a summary of what they've learned, I've developed a list of the essential components of a working succession plan. In every company where succession was handled smoothly and positively, each of these components was carefully thought through, developed, and successfully carried out. If any one of them is missing or poorly handled, the dream of smooth management transition is almost sure to become a nagging, low-grade nightmare.

If a family business is going to be truly successful — growing, profitable, and, above all, a happy place to work, year after year, generation after generation — this is what must happen:

1) *"Rich" kids have to be taught how to survive their dangerous opportunity.*

2) *Their spouses have to be integrated into the family as they arrive — a sometimes painful, but necessary, process.*

3) *A long-range business plan must be developed — "long-range" meaning farther ahead than next weekend.*

4) *The business plan must be followed — but it must allow enough flexibility to change as the world changes.*

5) *Successors have to be qualified — and then selected by some plan more formal than chance, default, or primogeniture.*

6) *A plan and schedule for management and ownership transition must be available — in writing (uncomfortably concrete though that might be for the present owners).*

7) *The present owner(s) must have realistic and practical things to do when the plan calls for them to let go — as it must.*

8) *Some outside body, call it an advisory council, an outside board, a management "cabinet," or what you will, must be given responsibility for all of the above — and its members must have the talent, energy, commitment, and courage to do the job.*

This kind of planning, not a separation of family and business, is the real road to success as a business owning family. It's often difficult and sometimes unpleasant, but like growing old, it's infinitely preferable to the alternative.

In the words of Confucius, the ancient Chinese family counselor:

Decapitation
Poor cure for headache.

DJJ
Cleveland, Ohio
December 1983

Section I

THE PLAYERS

Chapter 1
THE HEIRS AND SUCCESSORS
The Luckiest Break in the World . . .
Isn't Necessarily

> *Not easily do they rise whose*
> *powers are hindered by*
> *straitened circumstances.*
> **Juvenal**

Business owners' heirs are the seed corn of the future. They're the *sine qua non* of business continuity. They're the raw material of growth and expansion.

Yet, with all their value, they are among the most poorly husbanded major resources in the Western World.

It's bad enough that the next generation is poorly prepared. But they also face something much worse. At almost every turn, their struggles to achieve their hopes, dreams and expectations are thwarted. In far too many family businesses, the process of "successor training" is so misguided, so poorly thought through, and so inimical to the successful growth of the heirs being trained, that the primary effect is to throw barbed coils of confusion and misinformation in their paths.

This isn't to say they won't be successful — enough of them are, in spite of their experiences, to impress us with the strength and resiliency of the human spirit — but this educa-

1

tional failure makes life much tougher than it has to be, and unfairly diminishes their chances for success.

HEIR EDUCATION BEGINS AT BIRTH

The heirs' education begins much sooner than most of us realize or care to admit. Successor training isn't something that begins with a sixteenth or eighteenth birthday, or the first job in the store or shop. It starts almost at birth.

The sons and daughters of the business owner are his preferred (and, therefore, primary) source of future managers. That's to be expected — and it's a real advantage. Who else could say they've been able to train their staff from the cradle?

Too much, too soon? Not really. Not if we remember two facts. First, young people born into business owning families *are* potential managers whether they (or any of us, for that matter) like it or not. Second, a subject as critical to a family as the business it shares, is too important to be learned "on the street" — or from others who don't really understand. Subjects "taught" in our economic alleyways are too often taught too late in life by cynical teachers heavily biased by their own frustrations.

This is why the first order of succession planning for the business owner — first in both priority and chronology — should be incorporating the preparation and training of his next generation of managers into his long-range goals.

Does The Boss take advantage of the opportunity?

Well, no . . . but, you see, he has "reasons."

I've heard it more times than I can count: "We've never really discussed the business with the kids; we don't want to push them." Push them? Is that how we approach potential customers, by never mentioning the product? Truth is, most business owners can sell just about anything to just about anybody — except their business to their own kids.

Let's make the assumption that a major drive behind building a closely held business is to build opportunity for our heirs. That's nothing to be ashamed of, so why feel we have to hide the fact from the very people who are supposed to benefit from our work and our success?

The answer I usually get is that to bring it up is to put unwarranted pressure on the heirs. Better that they be spared that for a while, and have a chance to develop in their own way.

At first glance, this sounds reasonable, and many parents retreat behind this shelter of reasonability, but often it's only an expression of two related fears. They worry that their heirs — the hope for the future — will reject the business. But they also worry (and maybe this is their major fear) that the kids won't have the commitment to hard work and long hours that their parents feel is essential for success. The desire to come in, Mom and Dad reason, should come from the kids. How else can we be sure it's real?

As understandable as these worries might be, the resulting veil of silence is unfair to the heirs and to the business.

Why? Because the children are being denied a knowledge of their potential inheritance, while the business is being denied their interest and understanding. Every heir to a business owner follows a family business career path. It might not be conscious. It's surely not planned. But it's there, and it's followed by the vast majority of the heirs in business-owning families, almost from the day they first open their eyes. Ignoring it doesn't make it go away.

As soon as consciousness dawns, definitely long before the so-called "age of reason," business owners' heirs become aware of the family company. In their early years, the kids soak up their environment like sponges. They watch, and they absorb what they see without much critical judgment. They might have little basis for understanding and comparison — but they make comparisons nevertheless, and they do think they understand.

Dad and Mom might not be pushing the business on the kids, but that doesn't mean the kids aren't noticing the business. Quietly, in their own attentive way, they're getting their elementary management education. Unfortunately, it's not a very good one.

TEACHING THE "DARK SIDE" OF THE BUSINESS

They watch both of their parents, but mostly they watch their mothers because Dad is off beating the hustings for business. When Dad's home, he's tired, or cranky, or worse. They don't see him happy very often, and they sure don't get much of an idea what he does for a living. The only thing obvious to them is that what he does can't be a heck of a lot of fun — not if it makes him so miserable.

Dad, meanwhile, is busily playing the hero (and a little bit of the martyr). Even this wouldn't be so bad if he just kept it consistent. But his successes are shot through with worries. His highs are so high and his lows so low that the confused signals he gives off baffle everyone around him. When business is good, he rightly accepts all the praise and glory. When business is bad, there's nobody to blame but himself. Those are violent swings and the effect on him is disorienting.

Dad's battle is intense and unrelenting. He has no personal foxhole to dive into, no place to rest. Exhaustion takes its toll, but (he's a hero, remember) he hides all of this from his family. At least, he *tries*. Generally, he fails.

He says very little to his wife (he doesn't want her to worry), but, of course, she knows. She knows better than he, in fact, because she's not distorting reality through a dream — not as much as he is. So Mom's worried, too.

And so are the kids. They may not understand, but they miss little of what's going on.

What *is* going on? Well, sometimes Dad and Mom quarrel. Sure, what couple doesn't? But only the business owner and his spouse argue about "The Business." Around the corner, tucked away in their rooms, the heirs are listening and absorbing, and wondering about this terrible problem in their lives called "The Business."

If Dad happens to be a second-generation heir, instead of struggling with a new business, he's struggling with Grandpa and, maybe, his brothers and sisters. This is a little different. Mom's not worried so much about the wolf at the door as she is about that "old dog" in her husband's manger, and (how could she forget?) all those in-laws. If the kids notice a difference, it's probably that added wrinkle of extended family (mainly cousins) in their lives. But subtle differences don't much matter to the kids. What they see is basically the same as their first-generation counterparts: there's a terrible problem in their family called "The Business."

Little wonder there's been an endless series of wry cartoons drawn to the caption, "Someday, son, this will all be yours."

Family business isn't all problems, of course. There are good times, too.

Sometimes, usually on Saturday or Sunday, the heirs get to go down to the plant, or the shop, or the store. Does Dad finally use the opportunity to show them what he does? Nope. What he does instead is let them play with the trucks, or the typewriters, or move the inventory from bin to bin while he goes through the mail and writes cryptic notes to the help on the backs of envelopes.

Does he show them the fun he's having with the business? Nope. He can't because of his own conflicting ideas. He wants to protect them from some of the more unpleasant realities of life (like the "poverty" he knew so well), but he also wants their respect (not to mention admiration and appreciation) for how hard he works. He worries they won't understand that his fun has its roots in hard work, so he works while he lets *them* play. It's a great lesson. They manage to learn "reward" without "responsibility," while coming to see Dad as an unhappy workaholic. Sure don't want to emulate that kind of life, they decide. There must be a better way.

But even Dad can't spoil it all. The kids do see some benefits. There's money, of course, and the good feeling that comes from a family name that's well-known in town. It's on a lot of trucks, billboards, and newspaper ads. People know them and those people are impressed — most of the time.

Even these benefits have sharp edges, though, something that confuses the young heirs even more. Sometimes neighbors and friends are envious. Or they make assumptions, generally unfair assumptions, about the heirs' "having it made."

Family success can cause pain, confusion, and internal conflict for family business heirs, problems they generally have to work out for themselves if Mom and Dad won't discuss the business because they "don't want to push."

As all of this goes on around them, the heirs are building a picture of their family company and the effect it's having on their lives. And the color scheme of that picture isn't all brightness and pastels.

Too many young heirs emerge from this early period in their "career path" feeling threatened by the business, resentful of it, or undeserving of the silver spoon they find in their mouths — or suffering from a confused amalgam of all three, which is often manifested as a cynical acceptance of the available fruits of Dad's labor.

This is the sort of base coat on which most business owners' heirs paint their dreams and career choices. Small wonder a career in the family business doesn't stick the way it should. Too many heirs either reject it out of misinformation, or accept it for all the wrong reasons, planting the seeds of future career switches, sudden departures, frustration, and sometimes even a claustrophobic bitterness.

In family after family, Mom and Dad express surprise. "We can't understand it," they complain. "The kids want no part of the business." Or: "They just don't have any sense of responsibility. They think the business owes them a living."

It shouldn't be so surprising — not considering the quality of their "elementary education."

It's not often that heirs get a balanced and realistic picture of the family business and their potential roles in it. Consider their typical "career progression":

THE SUMMER JOB/"DEDUCTIBLE ALLOWANCE"

Almost everybody has a summer job sometime in their lives. For just about every heir to a family business, this generally means a summer job working for Dad. (Never mind that the kids might see their future careers elsewhere. A summer job is "different.")

Thus, new uses for the business are found. Either it's an excellent answer to the high unemployment rate facing the nation's teenagers, a tax-wise way to get some return for the kid's allowance, or a way to teach the value of hard work. Often, it's a little of all three.

For the heir, who doesn't know any better, it's either the assumed thing to do, the easiest path to take, or something over which they have no control.

None of these reasons or assumptions is invalid, of course, but neither do they demonstrate much thought being given to the fact that the careers involved are those of the next generation of owners. Hard, "dirty" work may be good training, sure, but is the family business the best place to get it?

Ask Dad, and he'll answer with one of his favorite precepts: "I learned the business the hard way, from the bottom up." To him, this seems a good enough reason for the heirs to do the same.

But is it? And are they actually learning what Dad did, the way he did?

These questions aren't often asked, but the answers are important. While hardly anybody would argue against the merits of entry level employment as a useful introduction to the realities of work, Dad firmly mounts blinders on top of his rose-colored safety glasses and makes all sorts of further assumptions of benefit — while studiously ignoring most, if not all, of the negative aspects of the deductible allowance.

I've heard all the justifications. I've also met hundreds of heirs and successors who've gone through this training, and my basic conclusion is that summer employment within the family business carries more potential negative results than positive benefits.

Some positive benefits are obvious. For example, a summer job *is* one of the fringe benefits of owning your own business — the ability to provide employment for one's offspring and other relatives. (The critics and harpies call this "rampant nepotism," but what do they know?).

But what about Dad's pet rationale — learning from the bottom?

Actually Dad *built* from the bottom, which is a significantly different experience from *starting* there. What he learned, he learned somewhere else. By the time he got around to starting the business, he had his hash marks and stripes. The people who saw him make his dumb, apprentice mistakes were in another company, maybe even another city (and they were probably part of the reason he left in the first place).

The heir, being availed of this great fringe "benefit" called the summer job, uses up his clean slate before he even realizes he had one. When he screws up — and he necessarily does — he does it in the full view and memory of people with whom he'll be working if ever he decides on the family company as a career. I've long believed there's a fortune to be made selling clean slates to family business successors.

And if building a clouded history isn't enough, the young heir is also often in a position to be manipulated by employees. The issue doesn't arise right away, but as the years pass, the "pals" the heir made in the early years have a hard time going from "Junior" to "Mr. Smith" — one of the reasons successors prefer the people they've hired over the old guard.

In short, that great institution called the summer job can have effects entirely opposite from those intended by The Boss. His intent is to present the business he's building to his heirs in the most effective way. Someday this will all be yours, he implies, but you've got to learn to ride it first. Too often, however, the kids never really get a sense of their inheritance. They don't look Dad's gift horse in the mouth — as Dad might complain. He doesn't give them a chance. He insists, instead, on showing them the other end first.

The good effects of summer jobs in family companies do exist, but they don't happen without planning and forethought. Working their first jobs with Dad, the heirs can finally have a chance to see him in action. They can see both his hard work and his enjoyment of it. They can also get their initial impressions of how much he knows, and how much they have to learn. They can see, first hand, how other people respect what their father does, and why.

But they don't see these things if all they do is shovel scrap around the machines, clean the troughs, type in the pool, count the inventory, or stock the shelves. These heirs are managers-in-training, not migrant laborers who pass with the westering sun. What they see, what they do, and who sees their mistakes all have an important impact on their future in the family business.

Summer jobs in the family company are probably here to stay. But just because we insist on doing something, we don't have to be careless about it.

WORKING SUCCESSORS: A SCHOOL OF NO KNOCKS

Summer jobs and adolescence (along with other mixed blessings of youth) pass inevitably into memory. Mostly, this change is a relief. But just as the heir moves on to bigger, more important things, he finds himself face to face with a harsh reality — the need to work for a living, to get a *real* job. Not too surprisingly, the family business suddenly begins to look a lot more attractive (read: "convenient").

Earning a living doesn't *have* to be disagreeable, and working usually isn't, not for those who've had good experiences in early jobs. If skills and talents are well matched to dreams and goals, working can be a joy. But most young people of 21 or 22 haven't had much chance to enjoy work or develop a real dream. They're just too short on experience and training. The economic world is still a new place, full of challenge and questions. This is the time for exploring that would, for testing limits and capabilities, and for expanding boundaries.

And it's therefore as much a time for anxiety and insecurity as it is for challenge. It's a time when a familiar harbor might look a lot more inviting than the open sea.

But sailors aren't made in port. Just as would-be sailors

need experience at sea, would-be managers need to learn the ropes in *real* jobs. Yet successors who start in their family company tend to get little training and even less responsibility — all of which has the negative effect of narrowing the probability of career "adventure." This allows the heirs a relatively safe alternative to facing the unknown. The heirs convince themselves it's okay to get their sea legs alongside the pier, that there's plenty of time to face the waves. Few of them realize the limitations they're exposing themselves to by taking their first "real" job in the same family business that brought them the summer job.

I put the word "real" in quotes because, in truth, the job most heirs walk into at this stage is (1) non-existent (if it were real, somebody else would already be in it), (2) unnecessary (with a limited payroll, who needs a "trainee"?), and (3) so poorly defined that the heir has no idea what to do (and worse, it allows Dad infinite latitude for redefining his expectations — no matter what the heir does, it's probably going to be wrong).

And here lie the limitations. By accepting this non-job, the heir not only sets himself up for frustration, discouragement and disillusion, but he also severely restricts his own training. In fact, it's difficult to find many examples of a business owner's son or daughter who served a management traineeship within the family's business and got the best training possible. Usually the opposite occurs.

Now, I'm realistic enough to accept the inevitable. Most heirs will, in fact, only work in their family business. But acceptance doesn't mean we shouldn't make the best of the situation. If they can't get their training outside the business, then we'd better make sure they're getting it within the business. We'd better be sure they're starting with a *real* job.

Of course, you say. Easy, you say. But is it? If it's so simple, why is the kind of job offered (and the career ladder it supposedly leads to) so often the last consideration when hiring heirs? Too often, the major consideration is the heir's age ("he's old enough to work"), which is seldom, if ever, in sync with the need of the business for an employee.

In reality, the hiring of family business heirs is done as a surprise, as though nobody knew the young son or daughter was actually getting older. Plan for their coming of age? Heaven forbid. We'll just rationalize hiring them when they show up at the door:

"It's a tough job market. Besides, where else could he start out with this kind of responsibility?"

Or:

"This way he won't have to waste his time learning about somebody else's business. The only business he needs to understand is *Ours*."

Or:

"We just plain need the help . . . and right now."

Let's take these one at a time, since they cover most of the rationalizations for hiring heirs without outside experience.

1) The "Real Responsibility" Argument. I've yet to see much compelling evidence that this justification is anything but self-delusion in most family companies. Sure, it's a tough job market. Finding a job has rarely been easy for someone with little or no experience. And if, in fact, the job available in the family company were a *real* job that carried an appropriate level of responsibility (and maybe even some training), it might be the best choice.

But is it? Not usually. Usually, the primary reasons for joining the family company are based on such rationales as the depressed job market, fear of the unknown, and because "it's there." The justification of more responsibility is just a semi-transparent gloss painted over the real reasons. The truth is hardly disguised, only clouded. The truth is, the company is unprepared for the heir (who is, in turn, unprepared for the company).

The most unfortunate part of the whole situation is that the heir-employee, in his naiveté, accepts the gloss as reality. For one thing, he wants to believe it. For another, he's too new and awed to question much of anything, including the reality of his job.

Dad plays the game well, too. So do the employees (who are they to buck The Boss?). On the surface, everything looks like non-fiction, but underneath, where it really counts, the heir is skipping down that yellow brick road to Oz.

There's no credibility at the outset and, therefore, no respect. As the student begins making the inevitable mistakes, the road to disillusionment (the heir's) and disappointment (Dad's) is direct and downhill.

And, finally, it's clear that the reason such highly touted responsibilities weren't offered to the heir on the outside is the evident fact that he or she was not yet qualified.

In fact, the key to developing a manager is not to *give* him responsibility, but to *prepare* him for it (and then increase it judiciously) — something often forgotten in a closely held company.

The acid test is to ask the question "Are we training a manager, or are we assuming we have one?"

Make-work jobs on the fringes of the organization — no matter how much everybody wants to believe they're "needed" — are no answer either. The *de facto* unemployment rate among private company "Vice Presidents of Marketing," "Managers of Business Development," and "Executive Vice Presidents" is staggeringly high and universally unrecognized — until the damage has been done. It's unemployment with a paycheck, but it's unemployment nevertheless.

It would be almost impossible even for an experienced non-family professional manager to survive a job like this. Because there's seldom any planning, any definition, or any agreement on what the objectives are, a manager put into this sort of job is forced to fly blind through a fog, hoping for a break. Eventually, he runs smack into Old Matterhorn, himself, and the makeshift airlift is over. At least an outside professional manager can learn and leave, chastened but wiser — as many thousands have.

But the heir is *family*. "Sure, it's his fault it didn't work out, but we'll give him another chance." For what? To fail, of course.

It's a neat dilemma. To stay means an uphill battle for credibility and responsibility, weighted down by mounting frustration. To leave means accepting defeat, antagonizing the family, and entering the outside world with even less confidence than before.

The only cure for this creeping paralysis is a real job, with real responsibilities, real performance standards, and objective evaluation.

2) The "Why Waste Time" Argument. For many families, it's a foregone conclusion that time spent working for somebody else is time spent learning things that won't be much help running the family business. After all, "our company is different."

What most business owners and successors fail to consider, though, is that tomorrow's family business is going to be different, too. Different from today's. Today's managers are fighting today's battles — a valid and essential activity. But the successor is intended as tomorrow's manager and he should be preparing to win tomorrow's war. He can't do that very efficiently in today's trenches.

An heir with an entry level "management" job in the family company too often isn't learning how to manage. He's learning management *history*. He learns to keep quiet, to listen, to watch, and *to stay out of the way*. During this period, he hears (and hears again) the war stories and gets "educated" as to why this company has been so phenomenally successful over the years. He learns there are sacred management rituals and secret understandings that bind the old guard together into a tightly controlled, mystical society dominated by a charismatic, if despotic, high priest.

To venture a question, even with temerity, is to risk a rending of the temple curtain and a lightning bolt across the brow.

Does the old guard teach? Nope. It *demonstrates*. The heir hasn't been around long enough to understand the subtleties and finer points. He's not initiated, so he can't join the ceremonies — and if (Heaven forbid) he's a *she*, the poor heir can barely expect to witness them.

The only route left is explanation, which is highly unlikely. Dad and the old guard never really had to think through what they do. Their management "style" evolved through a continuing process of mistakes, flurries of desperate activity, and survival. Management training under these conditions, when it exists at all, is little more than a series of loosely connected "just so" stories. "This, youngster, is just the way it is."

At least, working elsewhere, the heir is guaranteed a real job and the chance to learn and make mistakes in action, to form management theories and develop a business philosophy based on something more concrete than legend and fraternal mysteries. If the heir is going to begin in the family company, this same sort of opportunity has to be available to him. The "real" job is crucially important — making sure he gets it is a dual responsibility, his and Dad's.

3) The "We Need Him Now" Argument. As with any of these arguments, this one can be valid, particularly in companies that have never gotten around to forming a middle management. The smaller and younger the company involved, the more likely the heir *will* be needed — and the more likely it will be that the heir will have a real job.

Such timing is a matter of judgment, but one hard question must be asked. If the heir is brought in today to fill a gaping hole in our labor force, what price will we have to pay in cutting short his or her management training for the future? Will the heir become hopelessly mired in the mud of today's monsoon? Is that good for the business?

Questions like this can't be answered with certainty, but we can sense the right road to take. Family business heirs are potential owner-managers of *real* companies with *real* management needs. Whatever training they get, whether it's inside or outside the company, should, itself, be *real* — and, to the extent it's possible, the best available.

THE NON-FAMILY SUCCESSOR

So far, I've been concentrating on the "lucky" break being afforded the son or daughter of a business owner. What about the potential successor who's not related to the present owners? While sons or daughters are seen by the outside world as the "undeserving rich," this man or woman will most likely be seen as an "opportunist" or "predator" depending on whether the viewer is outside or inside the present owning family.

Whichever the case, notice how the successor's position is somehow considered undeserved. We've already looked at why the blood relative is undeserving, but what about the non-family successor, the *acquiror* of a closely held company?

It's not unusual for a business owner to find himself or herself with no family heirs. Sometimes this is simply because he lacks heirs. But it's also possible the children he has aren't interested (remember the effect of the early training), or he hasn't enough time to wait for sons or daughters to get ready.

Without family heirs, the business owner can take one of three steps. He can prepare the company for sale or merger, he can transfer ownership to successor managers on the present management team, or he can bring in an outsider who has the qualifications needed to run, and eventually own, the company.

If he decides to sell — assuming he *can* — successor management ceases to be his problem and becomes the concern of the new owners. On the other hand, if he decides to transfer to non-related insiders or outsiders, he may have the kernel of a succession plan in mind, but the process presents a wide range of serious issues that must be considered and settled — for the outsiders' sake as well as his.

There are some basic concerns to be considered and taken to heart — by the owner and the successors. If these facts of life are understood, mutually, the process of succession stands a much better chance of working.

1) Non-Family Successors Are Not Members of the Family. This might seem obvious, but we have to remember that the business owner looks upon his business as another

child, one he knows better than any of his other children (it o-
beys him better, too). Consciously or not, he looks upon any non-
family successor the way he would a son- or daughter-in-law.
This is more than just a business. It's *his* business — and he's
not going to give it away lightly, at any price.

For this reason, The Boss tends to extend his paternalism
from the business child to the new "in-law." In a sense, he feels
the prospective successor is, in fact, "marrying" into the family.
Given this assumption, it's a relatively logical leap to wanting
the successor to take part in family activities and to conform,
somewhat, to the family culture.

The successor is naturally flattered by this at first. After
all, the prospect of working into the ownership of a successful
business is a heady thing, probably something he or she has
coveted for a long time. Being included in the family seems like
a good way to cement the process. But what the successor sees
as "being included" and what The Boss sees tend to be very
different.

To the outsider, the relationship is a casual one — knowing the family members, maybe being included in an occasional
dinner, that sort of thing. The Boss, however, has something a
little more inclusive in mind. After all, it's his business that the
successor wants to walk off with. He wants to be sure of this
person's intentions, moral character, psychological stability, and
general conformance with the standards he's come to expect.

Essentially, The Boss is looking for evidence that the
prospective successor shares the family culture and values. No
matter that the chances of this happening are exceedingly small.
Dad knows he can bring the successor around. He begins to work
on this — criticizing certain personal behaviors, encouraging
others — with his usual lead-footed subtlety (a technique sons-
and daughters-in-law may also recognize).

The successor at first is only bemused by The Boss's behavior, but eventually begins to squirm under the pressure The
Boss brings to bear. What the successor thought was a business
relationship with social overtones, is becoming a personal involvement that overshadows the business altogether. Eventu-

ally, these personal misunderstandings become business misunderstandings, and the once starry-eyed outsider finds himself an outsider again — seeing stars of another kind.

The family/business relationship needs to be discussed and settled from the beginning. It may be that a close personal relationship is possible. If so, that's an added blessing. But this is unlikely and should *never* be assumed.

2) Heirs' Career Decisions Are Revocable. Sons and daughters of business owners are notoriously mercurial in their decisions about the business and their careers. This isn't because they're deliberately cussed or capricious. They're confused, for all of the reasons outlined earlier.

The business owner's ultimate commitment is to his family — something not peculiar to business owners, just more important to remember in their case. The Boss might be convinced that his sons or daughters have no interest in the business. They might be convinced, too. But these things have a way of changing, and this possibility has an important implication for the agreements between The Boss and any outside successors.

If the business owner is really certain of his children's intentions and expectations to do something other than come into the business, it's in his interest and the interest of the company to begin preparations for successor management as soon as possible. With this certainty, the business owner can feel more comfortable getting into binding contractual arrangements with non-family members (assuming, of course, that he's taken the normal precautions to assure competence, stability, and so forth). The outside successor who finds himself in this rare situation is fortunate.

But where there is uncertainty — which is more likely to be the case when the business owner's children are in their late teens or early twenties — decisions will have to be made in stages. First of all, it should be clear between the outside successors and the business owner that certain doors are being left open for the children. Secondly, Dad should frequently discuss the business and the future with his heirs to make sure they understand the narrowing options and to make sure he recognizes changes in their attitudes as early as possible. It's possible that the children will decide to come into the company. It's in ignoring this fact that business owners make some of their most serious mistakes with outside successors.

They assume that no professional manager in his right mind would join a family business when the heirs are hanging like swords of Damocles from the rafters. So they choose to ignore the "slight" uncertainty in their heirs' minds (while subconsciously hoping against hope that they'll change their minds). After all, The Boss figures, I have enough problems. Why create trouble where it doesn't (yet) exist? The potential acquirors, excited as they are at the opportunity, decide to ignore their own lingering doubts, assuming for their part that to raise the question is to queer the deal. All of this works fine until that sorry day that an heir shows up at the front door wanting a job.

Two facts must be admitted. The business owner *needs* to begin developing successor management as soon as possible. The process is lengthy, difficult, and prone to false starts. The acquiror-successors have a chance at a significant opportunity which shouldn't be taken lightly. But given all that can — and often does — go wrong, both need some sort of protection, designed carefully to maintain mutual flexibility in a changeable situation. This is the subject of Fact Number 3.

3) There Should Be a Written Agreement which Allows Mutually Beneficial Divorce at any Stage. Just as prenuptial agreements can smooth out concerns about getting married in later life, a "pre-succession" agreement can do a lot to ease the minds of both The Boss and the non-family successors — and their families.

Each is taking a significant risk. The Boss is hoping that the potential acquiror is, in fact, going to fit into the company. But he also has normal doubts about the wisdom of the course he's chosen. Is a non-family successor really such a good idea? Can he trust him (or her)? He wonders, too, just how sure his own children are that the business isn't for them.

The acquiror has concerns centering around the benefit he will be getting from the time and labor he invests in the owner-manager's business. This isn't a relationship like the primarily financial one between a manager and a major public company. Instead, it involves significant sweat equity investment on the part of the incoming successor. The business owner generally can't afford large cash outlays for management help, so the acquiror works at limited income on the presumption that someday it'll all be his — and then he'll get his rewards.

Well, at any stage in this process there are many things that can go wrong. Changing economic conditions might change the assumptions on which the agreement was based. There may be differences in personal chemistry, management style, or goals. Blood relatives might intrude. Spouses might not get along. Many bugs are lurking in the woodwork to nibble on what once seemed like a good idea, but most of them can be exterminated — if the acquiror and The Boss can avoid feeling trapped. It's *fear* of alternatives, not problems, that cause people to harden, become inflexible, and generally lose their ability to compromise intelligently.

How the acquiror and The Boss work out their "escape hatches" is really an individual matter, but such mechanisms as limited agreements not to compete ("non-competes"), restricted stock with fair valuation formulas, severance arrangements, and the like can help ease fears and concerns about issues not related to the central job at hand: increasing business profitability for everyone's mutual benefit.

This can be worked out in many different ways. Probably the most efficient approach is for the business owner and the potential acquiror to invest time *before* they start working together to list their objectives and concerns. Among the issues that should be discussed are:

a) *Compensation standards and determination.*

b) *Competitive restrictions to be placed on the acquiror in the event of "divorce."*

c) *Ownership or equity transfer intentions, schedules, standards, and restrictions.*

d) *Mutual and exclusive rights to jointly developed assets such as products, services, customer lists, brands, logos and other tangible fruits of the association.*

There's no harm, either, in discussing the nature of the social relationship the prospective partners intend, as well as any expectations they might have for their respective children. In short, if it's an issue that might come up eventually, it's best to bring it up at the outset, no matter how uncomfortable the discussion might be.

Often, the parties to the agreement convince themselves that bringing up particularly sensitive issues might ruin the deal at the outset, so the issues are buried "until later." That may be fine for getting the agreement off in the beginning, but the sore spot will remain — and only become more difficult and wounding later.

Becoming a business owner's potential successor may be a matter of being in the right place at the appointed time, but actually *becoming* that successor takes much more than luck. Following a business owner and becoming a successor owner-manager takes competence, diplomacy, tact, guts, hard work, sweat, hard work, competence, and hard work — not necessarily in that order. Oh, and hard work is important, too.

Having competent successors available to take over a successful company isn't a matter of being blessed. The business owner, in order to develop his relief management team, has to open himself where he's always been secretive. He has to narrow his options to one or a few unknowns. He has to admit to his limits and be able to accept the limits of his students. He has to learn to listen and to compromise.

Succession isn't luck. It's *planning,* careful planning, the first step in which is understanding — jointly, by The Boss and the heirs — that being a rich kid or one of the business anointed isn't all soft grass and hummingbirds.

Those who fail at the process deserve our compassion and understanding. It's a tough house to play. Those few who really succeed at the process richly and fully merit all the rewards they get.

Chapter 2
THE BOSS
"But Our Irresistable Force IS the Immovable Object!"

Nothing can be more disgraceful than to be at war with him with whom you have lived on terms of friendship.

Cicero

"Sure, it sounds reasonable and diplomatic to 'solve the Old Man's problems before your own,'" a successor's wife once complained to me after a seminar on succession. "But what if he just won't listen to *your* problems? What do you do when all he does is sit there like a huge block of marble, glaring at you and acknowledging nothing?"

Her husband, it seemed — despite his obvious frustration — was still willing to give The Boss another try. But his wife was in a different state altogether. She was impatient. She was bitter. And she was angry.

"I hate to say it, but I think we should bail out now," she said to her husband. "I don't believe this airplane is going any higher."

Maybe she was right — and then again, maybe she wasn't. But whatever the truth in her particular case, I recognized the sentiment she was expressing. How, she was asking, could she solve a problem with Dad if Dad doesn't even see it as a problem? More specifically, I guess, she was asking why she should keep trying.

There's no easy answer to "Why?". Motivation for staying in a family business has a lot of human and economic dimensions — the desire to make transition work, the opportunity value of the business, and the love and respect existing among family members — and I'll devote a lot of attention to it in Chapter 4. At this point, what's needed most is an understanding of the "what?".

What is it that causes all these problems between generations?

I've yet to meet a business owner whose intention it was to become a barnacle on the derrière of progress. The Boss usually senses that his standards, his values, even his dreams aren't entirely shared by his successors and their spouses, but he doesn't see the differences as fundamental. Time, he believes, time and experience, will bring them around. He doesn't do anything active because he doesn't believe it's necessary.

To the heirs, however, the differences appear fundamental, complete, critical, and seemingly unbridgeable. They've tried (or think they have) reasoning, pleading, arguing, cajoling, even threatening, all to no effect. They've tried "everything" and still Dad won't "change." What's left to them — short of managerial assassination, a bloodless coup, or outright desertion?

WHY DAD IS SO TOUGH TO MOVE?

Why won't the business owner budge? Is he naturally perverse, thoroughly enjoying the gnashing of teeth he's causing for his heirs and their spouses?

Dad's in-laws tend to believe this more easily than his children. Because his kids share their basic roots with him, they can often see at least *some* of his point of view (an open-mindedness their spouses see more as a handicap than as sensitivity or virtue). Shared culture is seldom enough, though. Dad's iron-studded, oaken barricade across the road to the future is generally very difficult for the succeeding generation to accept, much less deal with. What makes things worse is Dad's failure to even see the wall he's built. He wonders what all the fuss and complaining is about. As far as he's concerned, the only barrier is the heir's own slow and painful progress.

From Dad's point of view, things *are* progressing — more slowly than he would like, but progressing. The problem, if there is one, is the heirs' failure to understand simple things like the real world, and life, and what business is really all about. Dad is buried in problems. His eyebrows are continually being singed by the brushfires he fights every day. He's built a significant business despite all the odds against him and now his major occupation is the desperate fight to hold it all together in the face of chaos and creeping internal entropy.

He's seen it all before — economic downturns, steadily aging receivables, unethical competition, supplier and customer disloyalty, ineffective and uncommitted employees. What he needs are more hands than a Buddha, eyes in the back of his head, and the agile moves of an All-American.

And, most of all, he needs help.

But what does he get from his heirs? Complaints. Criticism. And, worst of all, suggestions on how to change the company and make it grow. My Lord, he sighs in the cluttered quiet of his office late at night, don't they understand how precarious this whole thing is? What I need is a little help fighting off the daily wolf that sweeps in with the mail. That's what needs doing. That's problem enough as far as The Boss is concerned.

And who's to dispute him? Over and above the fact that Dad has the swing, deciding, and conclusive vote, he's really not wrong. Most of the ideas and suggestions his heirs come up with do tend to increase the level of risk without seeming to offer a concurrent reward that meets *his* standards. He knows that great ideas mean work, and usually a lot more funds than are budgeted, but he already has more expenses than he can handle. These are facts.

Most would-be successors don't see this side of things. If they did, they'd use a lot more judgment in their campaigns to build and grow and change the company. Change is necessary.

Successors do need to build for the future and find ways to prove their talents. In this they're not wrong. Nor are their spouses wrong in wanting to see something happen. The problem lies in the way most successors (1) judge their own ideas and (2) try to gain acceptance for the best of those ideas.

The ability to judge the quality of an idea comes partly from experience. What seems to work? What hasn't worked? It's a skill that comes over time through risk-taking and neck-extending — the Real Job I referred to earlier. But what do you do when you don't have the experience? You do the same thing we're going to advocate for Dad to do: run your "great" ideas by objective outsiders with judgment.

Maybe the successor is fortunate enough to have access to an outside board, but if he isn't, he would do well to set up an "advisory council" of his own — peers, advisors, friends, anybody who can help analyze the quality of an idea without the handicap of having given birth to the thing.

But let's just assume the idea is good. The successor still can screw it up by fumbling on the packaging of that idea.

The most common "package" is the "idea-in-a-memo." The successor hatches a bright idea in the frustrated search for something interesting and challenging to grab onto, runs it with a few "eurekas!" by his or her spouse, then writes up a "seminal" memorandum sketching out the essential elements of the idea. This memo is then circulated to Dad and the key managers, and the successor sits back to wait for the accolades and kudos that are sure to come in response to such a brilliant stroke.

And what response is there? Usually none. If there is an answer, it's usually something on the order of a "Good idea . . . let's discuss AYC" scrawled in the margin. Well, of course, that means at *The Boss's* convenience, which seems to be seldom, if ever. He was too busy this week. Maybe next month after the Schmedly project is wrapped up. Or at the convention in April . . .

Basically, he really doesn't want to talk about the successor's idea at all. He hasn't the time — and even if he did, what's the point? There's no time for follow-through anyway.

The problem, as most key managers in a family business know from experience, is that there's no shortage of ideas with potential. This is true, in general, in industry all across the globe. What is in short supply is *implementation,* ideas that are actually transformed into working projects, products, or businesses. Too often, a growing business still in the "surprise" stage of success gets stuck reacting to events instead of planning to make events happen. If an idea is going to work and have any value, most of the support and logistical work — the planning — has to be done to make it work.

Most successors *want* to do that work. The problem is, it requires a long, direct flight through Dad's unconscious flak. That's a damned unpleasant prospect, one that's too easily put off. Thus the "memo." It's really a trial balloon.

What was in the successor's memo? "It would be a good idea if we were to . . ." The first and most active reaction the reader has to this sort of suggestion is to raise a jaded eyebrow to that heavily loaded world "we." We, who?

The "we" might be the successor's way of bringing others into "owning" the problem, but those others are more likely to read "you do it."

Pigheadedness, the successor will call it. Stubbornness. Hardening of the ambitions. Conservatism. There are a lot of phrases for this resistance from the power structure. And when the heirs come home mumbling about roadblocks and stupidity, some of what their spouses say couldn't be printed in a sailor's liberty manual.

Yet, if we were to blow away the fog of frustration, most every successor would have to admit nobody in the company would object to a successful new idea that would expand business, increase market share, and strengthen profits. *If it didn't cost anything.*

The problem lies squarely wedged in that abysmal crevasse yawning between the "good idea" and the "successful project."

Every venture begins with the intuitive leap, the "Idea," but that idea is only raw material. Business ventures aren't artistic creations composed in inspired solitude in a garret two flights above a soup kitchen. They are intimately involved in the changing world around them — and so must be their creators. Managers in closely held businesses — indeed, in businesses in general — manage *economic* creativity, which carries as one of its central premises the requirement that the creator also be an *implementer*. Ideas are useless in the economic world unless they result in positive economic results.

New ideas without good implementation are worse than useless, in fact, because they usually waste precious and limited funds, man-hours, and resources.

Take computerization. Now this is a crowded bandwagon. It's easy to get into. The machinery, pushed by all those eager, hardware-Chauvinistic salespeople, is all too easy to buy. The need can be demonstrated ("Just think, if we could get all the order processing on the screen, then all the "girls" would have to do is . . .).

Good idea. Sure. But why are there so many computer systems in family companies that are unused, under-used, abused, and just generally inadequate? Somebody had a great idea — with no real planning and little follow through. These expensive mistakes aren't the result of incompetence. Usually, they're the debris from too many flights of too many unconnected trial balloons.

Formulating an idea is only the first step in the process of business development. The major responsibility is the pursuit of that idea into economic viability. Ideas are as common as grains of sand. It's the crystallization of selected ideas into useful, viable results that makes an idea an IDEA.

UNDERSTANDING — AND MANAGING — RESISTANCE TO CHANGE

Implementation isn't everything, though.

Every family company has a state of the art, a level of business and risk that provides a base line from which every new idea diverges. To be viable, the new idea can't open new territory at too wide an angle from the status quo. This isn't a

limitation caused by parochialism. It's a dictate of common sense, defined by the limited resources available.

The job of the manager in this continuing change is making the necessary leap realistic, possible, and acceptable to the other people who will be involved in making it happen.

This requires much more than a memo and a sparkling, expectant smile.

For every improvement, Murphy or some other equally sagacious wit once noted, there is a natural and opposite resistance. The greater the proposed change, the greater the incline people are asked to climb, the greater will be the resistance — in all its forms.

People resist change. We could wish people would be more original, more open to change and innovation — but then again, maybe we shouldn't. Experience *does* teach a few things, and the fact that age tends to correlate with caution should have a message for each of us.

Getting that "immovable" object — Dad — to move isn't a matter of force. Threats or demands seldom work, at least not for long. Where successors have succeeded and where management transition has actually worked, the road their companies took was usually through territory where the *need* for change was greater than the built-in resistance to that change. Sure, that's a subtle point of balance, but a successor, like any effective manager, has to be comfortable with subtlety — and human nature.

What the successful "advocate of change" usually does is watch carefully for problem areas — unproductive departments, unprofitable products, exploding competition. Each of these increases the need for change. The trick is to be subtle enough and sensitive enough to feel when that need for change is great enough to outweigh the risk inherent in the idea proposed as a solution.

(Recessions have helped. When business goes sour, it's a lot easier to move into new areas, new ways of doing business. But few of us pray for recessions so we can change.)

Resistance can come from many directions. It can be the result of laziness and the plain refusal to see a problem because of the work required to solve it. Resistance can come from an individual's own concerns, high on the list of which is often the concern for security. Resistance can also be built into the whole culture of the family business — "This is the way we do things, this is the way we've always done things, and this is the way we will always do things. What works, works."

People have a lot of creative ways to avoid tackling a problem. Most of us have heard these statements before:

"Problem? What problem? I don't see any problem."
Or:
"Aw, that's nothing to get upset about. Let it go, it'll work itself out."
Or:
"Sure, I see the problem, but we can handle it with what we're already doing. No need to start reinventing the wheel."

Each of these statements will sound familiar to a working successor. Each represents the resistance that's built into people and organizations to new approaches and new ideas. And no one of them is inherently inappropriate, even though they may represent barriers to eager, aggressive young managers trying to make their mark on the company.

There are successors who've broken free of their frustration. Those I've known who've done it — and managed to get their business-owner parent to see value in their ideas — have usually been successful in two key ways:

1) *They've been able to understand the resistance they face, changing what they can realistically change, and living with what they can't change.*

2) *They've concentrated on practical, realistic implementation rather than blue-sky suggestions.*

To paraphrase Confusius, the journey of ten thousand miles begins with a determined sigh.

VALUES VS. FACTS — AND WHY THE
DIFFERENCE MATTERS

Sure, but how does one go about accomplishing that first part — determining what's realistically changeable? We still seem to be begging the question, because, to the successor, *nothing* seems changeable in *Dad's* business. He just doesn't see things the same way.

Is the "Generation Gap" really uncrossable? Sometimes it sure seems that way, as if the only way to bridge the chasm is to take the Evel Knievel approach — strap a Saturn rocket to your butt, throw a parachute on your back, slap on a helmet, close your eyes, dump the clutch . . . and hope.

That's a fairly hairy approach, particularly when the goal is something as serious as management transition and business succession. And, it usually doesn't work.

There is a better way. We've spent a lot of time studying family companies where at least a rope bridge existed between the generations. Communication may have been shaky and precarious, but it existed, nonetheless. And, once those first lines were thrown across and in place, they almost invariably got stronger over time.

How did the successful ones do it? Primarily, they discovered ways to tell the difference between possibility and desire.

Disagreements in family companies can be about facts — size of market, profit margin, potential costs — but they can also be about personal opinions — acceptable risk, levels of reinvestment, compensation systems — (which the theorists like to call "values"). Many of the problems in family businesses come about because of the inability to know what sort of disagreement is in progress.

Carrying this thought further, it's safe to say that "generations" don't disagree about matters of fact. Not usually. Instead, they disagree about opinions or personal values, but they *think* and *act* as though facts are at issue. This fundamental confusion is the most common reason why so many of the successor's "new ideas" meet with "resistance" from The Boss.

Maybe an example would help. This confusion between facts and opinion isn't just between generations, and not only in business. History is full of examples. A classic "values" conflict occurred between MacArthur and Truman over how the United Nations forces should respond to China's "intervention" in the Korean War.

The issue seemed simple. MacArthur believed the bridges over the Yalu River and even Manchuria should be bombed and neutralized, even if that meant a full scale war with China. Truman, on the other hand (along with most of the allies, members of the Security Council, and even the Joint Chiefs) believed war with China should be avoided. It was, in their opinion, ". . . the wrong war, in the wrong place, and at the wrong time, and with the wrong enemy."

A matter of strategy, one might conclude, arguable with facts and statistics, probabilities and outcomes. But if it were that simple, why did the conflict escalate to the point that a President of the United States felt forced to relieve a popular and capable commander in the field?

MacArthur and Truman weren't, in fact, disagreeing so much about the advisability of war with China as they were about their personal definitions of victory. Basically, they shared many of the same facts, but were totally at odds over personal values. MacArthur's values in the situation were summed up in his explosive letter to Rep. Joseph Martin in April, 1951. His closing words were "There is no substitute for victory."

Truman, on the other hand, along with most of the Western leaders, was equating wars for total victory with wars of mutual annihilation. For him, there *was* a substitute for victory — a negotiated peace.

This isn't the place to argue the relative merits of the two positions, but the example should help to emphasize the intractability of differences in basic values. Harry Truman found it impossible to reach agreement on a strategic decision with his commanding general in Korea, not because they didn't agree on the strategic merits of bombing Manchuria, but because they had totally different personal beliefs about the purpose for fighting the Korean War.

It's an unfortunate fact of experience that disagreements between The Boss and the heirs tend to escalate to the same level of confrontation. Even worse can be the "discussions" that go on among siblings in a second-generation business (or cousins in the third generation).

Successful management, business planning, and family harmony in general require agreeable decisions, and successful decision-making hinges around three basic factors:

1) The alternatives have to be understood.

As will be discussed in more detail in the chapter on planning, one of the first steps in long-range management is to do a "profile and analysis" to determine what the problem is, followed by a little brainstorming to come up with the available solutions. If, for example, sales are dropping (and everybody agrees that this is the problem!), some alternatives might include adding sales people, opening retail stores, creating a distributor network, or mounting a national advertising campaign.

2) The alternatives have to be narrowed to those which are possible for the company to accomplish.

While it might be possible to add a few sales people, a national ad campaign is often beyond the resources of smaller companies. Alternatives and possibilities are difficult to determine, but they *are* determinable with enough research and thought. More importantly, they depend on facts, and can usually be debated on a factual level without overwhelming difficulty.

It's actually Stage 3 of the decision process that causes family companies the most trouble:

3) Select the possible alternatives that are desirable.

Possibility is one thing. That's a matter of fact. Desirability, particularly given the power structure of most family companies, is a different matter altogether. Most people can differ reasonably on matters of fact. Matters of personal needs and desires — values — usually prove to be tough, however,

and fundamental. When the difference isn't even recognized —
as too often it isn't — reaching consensus becomes almost
impossible.

Management issues are heavily loaded with many different values components, but experience has disclosed four
major categories of disagreement:

1) Business Goals.

How one approaches management decisions can vary
greatly depending on what one expects for and from the business.

A business owner wanting to build a financial empire is
going to approach decisions quite differently from someone who
is only running a profitable hobby. A commitment to sales growth
is quite different from a commitment to return on sales, and the
two can quite often be incompatible — at least in the short term.

And these are only two examples from a list of possible
goals. What about product quality, private branding, diversifi-
cation, foreign marketing . . .?

2) Personal Goals.

In family companies, the desire some people have for
income stability and security often flies in the face of others'
desires for income growth and challenge. In many senses, these
are incompatible values — yet neither is right or wrong. It's
impossible to "prove" one over the other as the desirable way
to go, yet many arguments over business decisions are really
(and unconsciously, in so many cases) disagreements over growth
versus stability.

3) Acceptable Level of Risk.

At a consulting session, I once asked a successor and a
business owner to estimate the maximum amount of money their
company could afford to lose on a new venture. The founder
said they couldn't afford to lose a cent, while his son estimated
a quarter of a million dollars!

This wasn't only a disagreement over dollars. It was a
disagreement that arose from their different business and personal goals. A business owner in his 60's sees much less long-
term benefit in risk-taking than he did ten or more years ago in
his 50's. In his 40's he was much more comfortable with risk,

and in his 20's or 30's, it was probably his ultimate challenge. It might be that the successor is only expressing an attitude Dad, himself, held 20 or so years ago. But Dad doesn't hold it now, and he's not likely to, ever again.

4) The Keys to Business Success.

Businesses succeed for many reasons. Some make it on innovation. Others on brilliant management. In some cases, service to customers is the major factor, while others depend on low cost and efficient delivery. These are matters of life cycle, product/industry class, and markets — but they're also matters of personal strengths and preferences.

A company run by a technological wizard tends to make it on innovation more than any other factor. A company run by a brilliant salesman will tend to base a lot of its success on customer relations and service. Facts and the past say one way is better than another in a given company, which is fine — until the next generation moves in.

Successors walk into businesses built on the strengths and preferences of somebody else (The Boss), and agreement to continue focusing in this direction depends on whether The Boss and the successor share the same specific talent genes.

That likelihood, of course, is very small.

These are matters of management style, personal objectives, and fundamental beliefs. They can't be proven or disproved. Instead, they must be thoroughly explored, together, by all key managers in family companies as a necessary prelude to working with conflict and resistance. Shareholders and managers must, in short, quit the fruitless debates and concentrate on understanding their values differences.

A PROCESS FOR RESOLVING DISAGREEMENTS

What makes Dad seem like an irresistible force *and* an immovable object is his inability to accept the successor's "facts" as convincing arguments. What the successor sees as a necessary (if hopeless) reiteration of the realities of a situation, Dad sees as naiveté and an inability to listen to common sense. Both believe they are pushing facts, when, in actuality, both are standing firm on opposing values.

And neither understands what's happening.

There is no quick fix, no rope bridge that can be thrown in an instant over the "generation gap." Solving values differences in the family business is a process, and it takes time, commitment, and mutual understanding. Sure, specific disagreements can be solved on the spot, as they usually are, by Dad's tie-breaker, but that's about as viable a long-term solution to disagreement as martial law is to political dissent.

There are four steps or stages to working with values differences. You might call this a strategy for reaching agreement. If you're a successor, you'll look at it as a technique for moving the immovable and breaching the impenetrable. If you're a business owner with restless heirs, you can call it a way to knock some sense into "The Kid."

I. CAREFULLY DEFINE THE PROBLEM EVERY BODY SEES . . . AND ALWAYS KEEP IT IN VIEW.

Before getting mired down in a debate about, say, whether to expand the product line, it's a good idea to back off the "problem" and look at the goal each party to the debate is trying to reach with a solution. Manager A wants to increase sales. B wants to broaden the line as a defense against competition. C is afraid expansion will dilute service quality, and so resists it. Maybe D is just tired and wants to take the profits and run.

Looked at this way, it's easy to see why this company is never going to come to a shared judgment on expanding the product line. They're discussing the wrong issue, and have no idea at what point their ideas diverge.

Well, finding that "point," the common ground, is essential to discovering what the real problem is. Somewhere on every major issue there's usually a point of agreement between The Boss, the successors, and other managers in on the debate. It might be something as broad as all wanting the business to grow, or to stay under family management, or as specific as the need to increase return on investment.

Once the point of general agreement is defined, that also tends to define the problem — "All right, we all agree. So how do we do it?" Now, expanding the product line can be put into the perspective of the commmon goal. Will it get us where we want to go? Why? Why not? These questions, now, are matters of fact. But they couldn't even be brought up until the values issue was understood.

What if Dad doesn't see the problem? Maybe you don't either. Back off. Look for the personal objectives and the point of agreement. In short, find a problem that he does see and begin working from — and with — that.

The business owner, from his point of view, often finds it hard to get The Kid to understand the need to conserve cash or control costs or limit investment to ventures with minimum, calculated risk.

"He seems to think," Dad grumbles, "that financing's a bottomless well."

Rather than get involved in arguments over specific expenditures or investments, wouldn't it be wiser, here, to find a problem mutually recognized (such as low profits), and then look for ways to solve that?

II. GATHER THE FACTS AND DETERMINE WHAT CAN BE DONE.

Notice this says "what can be done," not "what *should* be done." The goal here should be to explore alternatives and determine which alternatives are possible for the company. It can be as free-wheeling a discussion as you want, because no value judgments are being made at this point. No ideas should be shot out of the sky or frowned into oblivion, because brainstorming about possibilities doesn't threaten anybody's value system.

Allow only one question: *Assuming we wanted to do it, could it be done* — could the funds be provided, the loan be obtained, the personnel be hired, the product manufactured, whatever?

And now comes the hard part:

III. DECIDE ON THE DESIRED ALTERNATIVE.

If everybody looks at the list of alternatives and one stands out above all the others, great. The problem is solved. If this doesn't happen — and it surely won't in every case — it's time to shift into a "values mode." Look very carefully at the competing alternatives, not for differences of fact, but for the underlying values differences they represent.

If, for example, the problem is declining profit on sales and one alternative solution involves investing in sales growth, while another involves raising price, this could reflect an underlying value difference between those who desire business growth and those who want business stability (a question of investment versus return). Define the seeming difference in values as well as you possibly can.

With this knowledge in hand, it's time to move toward a decision. There are four basic decision methods managers can use, and they're listed below in ascending order of desirability:

1) The Force of Events. If a company fails to make a decision, time will almost inevitably take care of the problem with an imposed solution. We have a problem with sales? Wait long enough and the problem will go away — along with profit, products, and the business.

Events, unfortunately, don't usually have the best interests of the business, or the managers, or the family at heart.

To paraphrase Thucydides, "A decision made this way can ruin your entire day."

2) Dad's Tie Breaker. This kind of decision making is admittedly very efficient. It carried Dad to the success he presently has. He casts his vote and then says, "anyone who disagrees with me can signify by saying 'I resign.' " Voilà! The decision is made.

In some cases of total confusion and disarray, this might be the best alternative. But that's in the short term. In the long term, it suppresses disagreement, discourages ideas, and demoralizes management — particularly the successors.

3) Compromise. I mean *real* compromise, not an enforced settlement like "Take me to Cuba and I won't blow up the plane." Compromise can work, but it isn't necessarily a good solution because achieving compromise often involves weakening the strongest points of the opposing alternatives, thus weakening each.

It's an accepted rule of thumb in mediation that you can tell an agreement is close at hand when both sides begin to feel they're being had. That may be the only way to mediate, but it doesn't do much to assure better chances for agreement in the future.

Still, barring a better basis for decision, compromise is better than nothing.

4) Use Outside Directors and Advisers. One of the proper roles for a working board of outside directors is to balance the values of the managers against the overall goals of the company. A well-informed board, presented with a well-defined problem, available alternatives, and issues in controversy, can be a great help in suggesting directions and moving management toward a solution.

If a working outside board isn't available (as, unfortunately, it isn't in the great majority of family companies — see Chapter 9), professional advisers can help fill in for them. Objective, capable outsiders will almost always provide a useful perspective to help the insiders see beyond their own disagreements to the best decision.

IV. AUDIT RESULTS AND RECYCLE WHAT'S LEARNED.

One thing is sure, if the issue is important enough to the company, a decision will be made, one way or the other. What we'd really like to accomplish is making future decisions easier and better. This is done by expanding the data and experience base used in making those decisions.

The way to do this is to record clearly the alternatives discussed, the value differences involved, who took what position, how the decison was reached, what results were expected, and how they will be measured. Then, follow up, regularly and honestly.

Did it work out? If so, why? If not, why not? What do

the results tell us about whether or not the alternative chosen was the right one *to help reach the agreed-upon goal?*

There's no real need to make this audit personal, not in any formal way at least, but everybody involved in the decision should honestly assess his or her role in the outcome and objectively note the relative value of everyone's contribution to the result. Errors in judgment as well as clear-sighted analysis should be acknowledged. An outside board can be a big help here, too.

Tie values to results, and tie results to an agreed overall objective. The process may sound circular, but it isn't. It's more of a spiral that constantly recycles honest differences with measured results to move toward a convergence of values.

HOW TO HOLD A "BLOODLESS" FAMILY MEETING

Does the prospect of a family or shareholder meeting leave you logy and listless? Does the prospect fill you with dread. Does the experience itself leave you prostrate?

If so, you're not alone. These are the typical results of attempts by shareholders and/or family managers to sit down around a table and come to decisions. Red faces, and even tears, often punctuate what is supposed to be a rational discussion of some important topics. Sometimes, family members simply decide to avoid the meetings. They're too painful.

Well, this state of affairs can't be allowed to continue in any family company. To put it bluntly, it's a dangerous situation. Left to itself, it will only deteriorate.

"But we've tried so many times," you're tempted to complain. "It *never* works."

Having attended and participated in my share of shareholder/family meetings, I understand the sentiment all too well. I've been surprised by the vehemence and suddenness of negative reactions. I've been frustrated by the lack of progress, the rambling, aimless discussions, and the meetings dominated by one individual. I've dragged myself home tired, depressed, and angry from meetings that seemed more to confuse than clarify problems.

But I've also moderated meetings that *worked,* sometimes for the first time in years. I've experienced the real kick you can get out of watching bright people wrestle constructively with a difficult problem. Decisions can be made, and every party to those decisions can win. Discussions can be rational and productive. And, yes, meetings can also (almost) be fun.

What's the difference between good and bad meetings? Usually, a simple matter of finding a structure that helps eliminate the "evils" that turn family/shareholder discussions into disasters:

1) Lack of an agreed-upon agenda.

While many meetings lack any agenda at all and wind up aimlessly looking for a direction in which to go, the agendas that do exist too often have no relationship to the "personal agendas" of the participants. And when people disagree with the choice of a topic, or have no interest in it, or believe discussion is fruitless, the discussion will, in fact, prove fruitless.

2) Lack of a disinterested moderator.

Even with a good agenda — defined as one that everybody agrees is a good agenda — most meetings have no effective "moderator," someone whose job it is to keep the discussion on track and productive. Generally the "chairman," who's usually The Boss, has that job. But whoever the moderator might be, he usually fails at the job. Why? Because he or she is involved and even embroiled in the discussion. Who can keep an eye on the tracks when fighting for control of the train?

3) Lack of participant "protection"

Ever bring up a good idea or suggestion and have everybody team up against you like a crazed motorcycle gang? Ever bring up another good idea or suggestion in that group? An intellectual "bodyguard" can be a great comfort.

4) Lack of a process for analysis and decision.

The "process" most often used is to throw an issue on the table, assume everybody has the same understanding of the problem, discuss the first solution suggested, reject that, then table the issue because it's too controversial. Next item?

5) Lack of a useable, functional record.

It's not uncommon to stop in the middle of a discussion and try to remember what the original issue was. ("Didn't we already discuss that?" "But that's not the point!" "I suggested that hours ago!") The minutes of these meetings — if there are any at all — usually read like the first draft of a James Joyce novel.

Each of these "evils" can be addressed and minimized, if not totally eliminated, by some relatively simple procedures. Each family and each company will have its unique approach, and that's okay — as long as the following basics take place:

1) Get agenda suggestions/comments from everyone prior to the meeting, make last minute adjustments at the beginning of the meeting, and set the next meeting's preliminary agenda before adjourning.

The key issue in making an agenda workable is making sure everybody agrees that the agenda is right. This isn't something that's submitted to majority vote. In fact, a well-run meeting should come to consensus, not a vote. When the agenda is right, everyone will know it.

2) Appoint a moderator, give him/her the agenda to protect, defend, and implement, and FORBID any participation by this moderator in the discussion.

This "moderator" is the keystone of a successful meeting. His or her sole concern is making the meeting work — by following the agenda, by setting time limits for discussion, by keeping the discussion to the process (see below), and by defending the rights of everybody to be heard without attack or personal criticism. *Any* involvement by the moderator in the discussion removes objectivity and destroys the natural authority delegated to the referee. Since it's a tough role that takes an interested participant out of the discussion, the moderator job should rotate, meeting to meeting.

3) Charge the moderator with the defense of each participant from the wrath, ridicule, or derision of the others.

As a non-participant and referee, the moderator is in the

right position to keep people off each other's backs. This role
should be emphasized up front, and personal attacks should be
identified in full view. "Charlie, you're attacking Marie. Cut it
out." Or: "Dad, we're brainstorming, which means no discussion
until all the ideas are brought out. Knock off the criticism."

**4) Divide discussion of each issue into problem
analysis, solution brainstorming, solution analysis, and
solution selection — and charge the moderator with
keeping the process on track.**

This process is central to making progress. Stick to it and
do things in order.

First, what are the components of the problem? What do
we have to solve? Make sure everybody agrees.

Second, what *could* we do about it? Just throw out ideas,
here. Brainstorm. List alternatives and hold everybody's critical tongue until everybody's exhausted the possibilities.

Third, discuss and narrow the alternatives. What's possible? What's impossible? What feels right and what feels wrong?

Fourth, come to a decision on the narrowed option list.
Try for unanimity or general consensus. If that's not possible,
vote. If all else fails, The Boss can break the tie. But decide.

**5) Appoint a "secretary" to keep a running re-
cord of the discussion in full view of the people in the
meeting.**

The best way to do this is with a flipchart, marking pens,
masking tape, a blank wall, and an objective writer. The secretary (who can be rotated every hour or so) is, like the moderator, forbidden to enter into the discussion. He or she has only
one job — keeping a running outline of the discussion. As each
sheet fills up, number it and tape it to the wall for everybody
to refer to and draw from. Later, this collection of ideas will be
used to generate the minutes. (There's an additional benefit,
here. Everybody tends to focus their attention on the record,
rather than on each other. That's a great help in depersonalizing
the discussion — and keeping everyone's eye on the ball.)

These are general principles for running successful
meetings. They work. If you want to get into the subject in more

detail, a good start would be "How To Make Meetings Work," a book by Michael Doyle and David Straus (Wyden Books, 1976), whose ideas provided many seeds for the above discussion. But whether you explore the ideas further or not, make sure you keep to the spirit as you adjust them to fit your family and your company. Above all, *try* them in the next meeting. You're likely to be pleasantly surprised at the results.

Nobody is really immovable. No idea is really irresistable. It just seems that way some times. It's entirely possible, of course, that the values of the successors and The Boss, or the goals of the cousins, or the spouses won't agree. But they can be helped to converge over time. They almost surely will if the process is honestly followed, some objective moderation is brought in, and reality is allowed to temper convictions.

Whatever is done, however, decisions must be made. Settling for conflict, frustration, or disappointment has no place in a family business — not, at least, in one which everyone agrees should survive and grow.

Chapter 3
THE "HEIRS-IN-LAW"
"He (She) Could've Done Better"

*A young man married is a man
that's marr'd.*
Shakespeare

What is it about our sons?

Do they have some genetically ingrained addiction to greedy, aggressive females?

And what about our daughters? Is it their inevitable compulsion to marry lazy, obnoxious, ne'er-do-wells?

Of course not. To hear business owners talk, most sons and daughters exhibit an appalling lack of matrimonial taste, but, in reality, they're complaining about the rough time they have getting along with their sons- and daughters-in-law.

The complaint is mutual, but when asked who's at fault in the whole mess, each "aggrieved" party points promptly to the other. They can't agree on that — nor can they even agree about the actual seriousness of the conflict. For the Son- and Daughter-in-law, the situation tends to go from difficult to un-bearable — mostly because Dad doesn't take things seriously. What I've heard over and over again from successors' spouses is "He (Dad) doesn't even see the problem." For The Boss, it seems, things merely go from nuisance to damn nuisance — and not much farther.

The Boss's in-law problems never quite become acute. Instead, they settle into a state of chronic annoyance, which he endures in the stoic belief that discomfort with one's in-laws is a natural part of family life (the way aching joints are borne as an inevitable curse of old age).

This is unfortunate, both from a human and from a business point of view. Ignoring festering disagreements can make life difficult and uncomfortable, but when a family business is involved, the *laissez faire* approach to sons- and/or daughters-in-law can lead to the breakup of a company.

This might seem like an exaggeration, but it isn't. Few business owners (and even fewer sons- or daughters-in-law) recognize the influence inherent in the position of the successor's spouse. The fact is, other than Dad, the person with the most power to determine the kind of future a closely held business is going to have is the successor's spouse.

Influence is often a matter of position, and there are few positions more inherently powerful than sleeping with the prince (or princess). It's a combination kitchen cabinet and bedroom boardroom with a very exclusive membership. When the last words about or against the king are said at night, they have hours of silent darkness to work into the successor's rather unstable psyche. Dad's got no voice, no vote, and no veto. He doesn't even share the platform. Over a period of years, those last words can build up into a swelling tidal wave of revolutionary rhetoric.

Dad might believe he can ignore his in-laws, but we would all do well to look a little deeper into the problem — if, that is, we're interested in preserving the future of our family companies.

FOUR BASIC MODELS OF "SON-IN-LAW"

The Boss's son-in-law usually comes in one of four basic models. If the business owner wants to maintain a productive, harmonious relationship with his daughter's chosen mate, he'd do well to understand the viewpoints and concerns of the particular models in his family "garage."

Most commonly recognized is the "Vice President" who is married to the Boss's Daughter, or the son-in-law executive in the family business. I won't say much about this fellow here, because his problems in actually working for Dad aren't all that different from the problems a son or an outside "acquiror" would face.

One major difference exists, though. That's the common prejudice that he's little more than an economic gigolo, using marriage to further his career. This problem isn't insurmountable for him, but it sure can be difficult. Competence and a high performance level tend to be specific cures, but even with talent, he faces an uphill battle in his wife's family company. Each degree of responsibility is grudgingly given in an arena of over-scrupulous review.

The second model, as yet somewhat rare, but growing in numbers, is the son-in-law working in the family business whose spouse, the boss's daughter, is the designated successor or "crown princess." This poor fellow combines all the problems of working for The Boss with the further problems of being the successor's spouse.

The most significant point to note about this difficult dual role is his need to solve a wide range of problems that tend to be "perpendicular" to each other. Surviving, here, requires a very resilient and flexible ego, with the assertiveness to carve out a real role in the business, all the while maintaining the sensitivity to support a spouse who's also a fellow employee. That's a lot to ask of anybody, and The Boss would do well to have a lot of patience with this young man. At least recognizing and acknowledging the complexities here is a very important step for all involved.

Model Three, also rare but steadily increasing in numbers, is the husband of a Daughter-successor who isn't, himself, involved in the family business.

The unique issue with this fellow is related to his career. When and as his career needs conflict with his wife's, he winds up in conflict with her family. It's often expected that his career will assume second place to his wife's, and too many business owners choose to ignore the fact that this is a priority with which he may not agree. One thing is sure. Whatever priority is set will have to be understood by and agreeable to everybody involved — and this requires discussion.

The fourth, and most common, son-in-law model is the son-in-law who has his own career, be it grand or not so grand, and who is married to a boss's daughter who, herself, wants nothing to do with a career in the family business.

This young man, assuming his father-in-law follows the most common (if generally misguided) approach to estate planning, is married to a potential minority shareholder. His culture places him in the role of "champion" of the rights of his spouse, so he's very interested, by marriage, in the progress of the business. Dad may not think he has much reason to care, but he does — and he will.

If his career is in business or one of the professions, he's bound to be even more interested — by personal inclination — in the actions of the family company. As a professional, he tends to be an activist, too. He's more or less used to being assertive. He understands the ebb and flow of funds and the fundamentally neutral ethics of the business world. He's not likely to be satisfied with platitudes, bromides, or obfuscating flak. And his trust is even harder to earn.

Whatever model a given son-in-law represents, he's an important person in the family structure, someone who is deeply concerned about decisions being made for the future of the company. Contented, he can be a loyal friend. Unhappy, he may be a formidable opponent indeed.

THE REAL PROBLEM WITH DAUGHTERS-IN-LAW

As important as The Boss's sons-in-law are, the most important (and difficult) spouses of business owner's heirs are the wives of successor-sons. These are the Daughters-in-law of The Boss (capitals mine).

(True, the number of daughter-successors is increasing steadily. In fact, it's almost an explosion — and a welcome one. This means, of course, that the ranks of successors' HUS-BANDS are swelling as well. Nevertheless, the statistics remain heavily skewed toward male successors, and they'll stay that way for a few years to come. The following discussion, therefore, will be about the wives of these successors, but it's worth noting that most of the "hers" appearing below could just as well be seen as "hims." Problems relating to the successor's spouse are not particularly gender specific.)

Once The Boss's Daughter-in-law has entered the business-owning family, it seems to take her almost no time at all to develop a "bad press" among her in-laws. Somehow, despite her initially pleasant personality and good intentions, she seems almost inevitably to get the role of a scheming assassin of family peace and harmony.

Most everybody is surprised by this turn of events, including her.

Her new role doesn't do much to enhance her image. Here's how I usually hear it: "Our sons, from the time they were this high, got along like you wouldn't believe. They played together, they were close. You couldn't tear them apart. When they got older it was the same. They worked together like a real team . . . *until they married those damn women!*"

To Dad, the problem might seem obvious. It's *her*. But we have to ask *why*?

Some of this is explained by her history; even more is explained by her experience with the new family. From her point of view, she *tried* to be nice, but almost from the beginning she was shunted off into a corner, some dusty niche well outside the normal family traffic patterns. Her in-laws tended to ignore her — when she wasn't being patronized, that is.

Oh, The Boss will say he tried to get to know her in the beginning, but she "wanted no part of it." She was stubborn. She was opinionated. She was even disrespectful at times. She just didn't fit in, but that was her fault because she trusted nobody.

"If she doesn't trust me," The Boss is likely to ask, "why should I bother with her?"

Even when he admits it's in his interest to try to open lines of communication with her, he's so hurt and distrustful himself that the "dialogue" he starts usually takes the form of a unilateral scolding and an attempt to "explain" reality to her. She, in turn, takes this (quite rightly) as a stiff pat on the head and the pressure in the family business cooker builds.

"What else can I do?" Dad grumbles, deciding to avoid the whole problem and leave her alone. She's her husband's problem. Let him tell her how it is. Thus does the "problem" filter downward in the family hierarchy.

And how well does the successor do as her educator? Terribly. In the first place, the situation is already explosive by the time the business owner's son gets the teaching job. But that's not all. The heir has his own problems and disagreements with The Boss — and who else does he have to talk to about those problems other than his wife? He's expected to pacify and placate the very person he needs to provide sympathy for *his* problems with The Boss.

He can't mediate because he's in the middle of the battle. Dad's not listening to his ideas. Nor is Dad giving him any responsibility or letting him take any risks (nor paying him what he's "worth," for that matter). How's he supposed to convincingly explain and defend a family business that's causing him so much grief?

Actually, he *does* talk about it a lot — at first: "Dad said 'No!' again." "He just doesn't respect my ideas." "We're always fighting." "He resists everything I want to do, overrules the decisions I make without him, and gets annoyed when I ask for his ideas."

Well, who else can the successor tell about all this? He knows at least his wife will understand.

And she *does* understand — all too well. Problem is, she gets only half of the story, the bottom half.

Her spouse, the successor, feels his love for his father and his family. He knows the love is a constant through all of the problems and frustrations, and it's the fertilizer of his hope and belief in the future. Sure, he's frustrated, but deep down he knows it'll all work out. Is this what he explains to his wife?

Nope. He doesn't get around to it, or can't, or just assumes she'd think it's silly.

Well, she's tough. She's resilient, to be sure. She hopes for the best. She's patient and supportive. But she's also human. Eventually, after months, perhaps years of this, instead of the understanding the successor expects and certainly needs from his spouse, he gets exasperation and growing anger. More and more frequently, she explodes in frustration that he doesn't stand up for his rights.

Even if he wants to play the peacemaker and forego his "sounding board," he can't. It's usually too late for that. She's been his confidant for years already. She knows what he thinks about Dad. She's heard it all, and now he wants to come and defend the old guy. Try again.

Almost without his awareness, things stopped being simple long before her anger showed. By the time he wakes up, business has become confused with personalities, love is mixed up with demands, and cooperation seems inseparable from sacrifice. Suddenly, he finds that their goals conflict and their values clash, generating an intense heat that seems to split everything into "us" and "them." As more time passes for the successor and his wife, the family business becomes the perennial winner of their Touchy Subject of the Week Award.

Instead of planning their future together, the successor and his wife always seem to end up talking about that "old @#*!%" and what should be done to force him to do what he's "supposed to." The successor has anxieties. She has fears. He advises patience. She wants results. All this turmoil keeps them pretty busy — going around in circles, getting nothing done.

As time passes, conversations escalate. The hurt Daughter-in-law asks more and more difficult things from her husband who feels he's stuck in a position between her and The Boss. He answers her righteous argument with a patient (and fatal) "But, on the other hand, look at it from his point of view . . ." and the mercury really begins to fulminate.

The would-be successor, trying to fit a little bit into both camps while mediating between them, dodges ineffectually in the crossfire. After a while, he begins to forget who the good guys are.

His conclusion from all this? Same as Dad's. It's useless to explain. Better not bring up the business at home anymore.

Which, naturally, makes matters worse.

HER PROBLEMS — AND SOME SHE CAUSES

In a family business, the life of the successor's spouse can be confusing, frustrating, and, in some senses, frightening. Her destiny seems to be in the hands of a despotic father-in-law, against whom her White Knight seems unable to stand. Most outsiders don't understand this, thinking she has it made — a view shared by her in-laws, who also see her as having a lot more than she had before.

Her spouse is the heir-apparent to economic royalty. With this connection to "wealth," her resources are assumed to be endless (and, of course, "undeserved"). She watches friends of many years become more aloof and distant with their growing assumptions of her increasing wealth.

As if this didn't make her lonely enough, she and her husband inhabit different worlds. His is the high pressure business world. He faces challenges every day, experiencing the excitement of success or the depression of failure. And, at night, he comes home exhausted.

If she has a career of her own, her successes, her failures, even her exhaustion don't seem as consequential as his. Not to his family, anyway. Her job (rarely it is a "career" as far as her in-laws are concerned) just adds another dimension to the problem. The in-laws seem to demand that she be superhuman in supporting her spouse. As she sees herself in their mirror, she's never caring enough, or domestic enough, or unselfish enough to allow her spouse unlimited time and energy for his work. After all, he's working in THE BUSINESS.

But even if she doesn't have a career outside of the home, and she focuses her attention and energies on the critical and important jobs of homemaker and mother (one of the few genuinely gender-specific problems), her increased "acceptability" to the family hierarchy does little to ease her frustration. She feels she's chosen a partnership with her husband, adding a domestic stroke to the economic oar he has in the water. She wants, needs, and deserves to know what's happening in the business.

She wants to find out how his day was and why the company is draining him of all his energy and spirit. But he doesn't want to talk about it, remember, which leaves her in the dark. Her needs aren't filled, while what's expected of her never seems to diminish. She's expected to be understanding, supportive, tolerant of his absence, and forgiving of his oversights. If she has a complaint, she's expected to swallow it to keep peace in the family. If she doesn't understand the business, she's expected to love it anyway. If she has worries or problems, she's expected to keep them to herself so he won't be burdened.

If she hesitates or objects to any of these expectations — which, because she's human, she almost inevitably does — she becomes "uncooperative," "obstructionist," "obnoxious," "aggressive," and "greedy."

She begins to believe that her husband's whole family is all too ready to see her as an interloper, maybe even as another one of her husband's "unfortunate" mistakes.

Instead of being integrated into her new family, she becomes "that woman." Hence my only half-facetious nickname, "Mata Hari."

The silent supportive role expected of the daughter-in-law is a carryover from a culture that really no longer exists. No matter how much Dad or Mom might wish it otherwise, young women of today want no part of that kind of feudal society. Today, women tend to see their personal lives in terms of mutual agreement. They consider themselves individuals with the same kinds of needs and rights as their spouses. They want to be acknowledged as persons in their own right and given the same respect given to anyone else.

WHY DAD CAN'T UNDERSTAND

Few problems in the family business are single-faceted, however. Dad's got a few shots of his own to fire.

The business owner would say that he has no objection to seeing women getting involved in business. He's smart enough to know that's inevitable. What he does object to, however, is their opinion that marrying an heir somehow gives them a say in how the family business should be run. He also believes he's being unfairly blamed for problems the heirs might be having, and resents being resented for what he considers to be kind and generous actions.

Dad knows life is tough. He knows he's done nothing but work his tail off for a quarter century or so, building the business that suddenly now has become the symbol of his "tightfistedness." This gets him upset, because, in his eyes, he's given up a lot in his life so that the women around him can have a good and comfortable life.

What hard work should bring, he believes, is some peace and quiet, and support from the people who are reaping the benefits of what he's built. Instead, what he gets is criticism and accusations that he's not being generous enough, or trusting enough, or that he's too duplicious about his plans. And to top it all off, he's accused of not taking his Daughter-in-law seriously.

Well, let him tell her a thing or two:

"You don't understand — probably never could — what this business means to us. You don't have any commitment to it and want everything now, things that my wife and I took years to build. Instead of supporting your husband, you seem to spend all of your energy causing trouble."

Dad resents this. He believes everything he's done and everything he's doing is building the future for his spouse, his children, and his grandchildren. Without him, he's convinced, that future just wouldn't exist. So how can his Daughter-in-law believe that he's standing in the way of his son? The heir needs to learn, and that takes time. Dad can't be replaced overnight.

And as to her complaints about his demanding too much of the successor, of there not being any time for home or family, his response, from the heart, is that this is the way it is. Period. If it weren't for that "demanding" business, there wouldn't even be a home to go home to.

Dad resents his Daughter-in-law's resentment that he has control over the company. *It's his company*! Worse yet, she not only wants a say in decisions, she thinks she has a *right* to that say. She might try to explain that he's got that wrong, that she thinks her *husband* has that right, but Dad won't accept that. He knows a Mata Hari when he sees one.

Dad, with his sense of greater experience and rectitude, tends to be an autocrat. He takes a parental role with his heirs and their spouses, and expects (almost dictates) certain behaviors and beliefs. The heir has years of experience living with Dad's peculiarities, but his spouse does not. She has no proclivity, in other words, to say "yessir" whenever that's required, because she doesn't *know* that Dad's heart is in the right place.

As one business owner said to me:

"You don't know how upsetting it is to spend all the time and energy I spend on this business, only to have one of these young women call me selfish or egotistical. They take the gift I've given them — a solid business — without so much as a 'thank you.'

"At the risk of sounding like some kind of Chauvinist, I don't believe wives should get involved with their husbands in a business. It's just too explosive."

Since Dad and his Daughter-in-law share neither genes nor childhood nor common experience, they clash.

After a few unsuccessful early attempts to "educate" this woman his son married, Dad decides he should maybe ignore her. She'll understand eventually, he figures, and will adapt to the program like everybody else.

Unfortunately, this is about the last thing she'll do — mainly because she expects *him* to do the adapting and understanding.

The inevitable result of all this waiting for the other guy to change is a problem that gets worse while everyone waits, heels in ground, for some magical change of heart. Nobody even attempts preventative maintenance (their righteous protestations to the contrary). In time, the situation becomes almost impossible.

HOW THE SUCCESSOR GETS STUCK IN THE MIDDLE

Most any objective outsider, meeting and talking with a frustrated Daughter-in-law, sees something much different from Dad's characterization of a greedy, aggressive female. What the outsider will most likely see is an insecure, uncertain young woman who doesn't understand the new life she's gotten into with her husband. All she seems to get are promises and assurances from Dad (when he talks to her at all) that everything is being done for the best. What she gets from her husband, on the other hand, only adds to her confusion.

In the early days of his apprenticeship, she heard his frustrations and complaints. She countered his feelings of inadequacy. His conversation was limited mostly to disgruntled monologues about Dad — what he wouldn't do, teach, let go of, spend, or understand. Later, as the successor sees the widening rift between his wife and his family, he resorts to evasive silences or attempts careful handling and peacemaking. Too late he tries to undo the damage largely brought on by the pain of his early days in the business. Through his innocent complaints, he's encouraged her to become an unstoppable champion — and through his "diplomacy," he's deprived her of an objective view of the whole truth.

What the successor finds is a spouse who seems to turn more and more against The Boss over time. If he thought he was in a difficult position before, his wife's new anger can make it almost impossible. He wants to stay with the business, but finds himself carried along by a powerful emotional current to the point where he may have to choose between his wife and the company.

He's in the middle. His wife has legitimate concerns for her family's security, his career, and their future together. Opposing those concerns squarely (or seemingly so) are The Boss's worries about the future of the business and how it impacts his own future.

The successor is the key to each of their futures, but the "solution" he represents is very, very different for each. It might seem obvious that the basic answer for everybody is the success of the business, but it's not that easy. Nobody agrees on the definition of success.

Eventually, almost inevitably and after a long time smoldering under the wallpaper, the conflict breaks into the open. With the opening of hostilities, a most important line of communication in the family — and the business — parts like an undersea cable in an earthquake. Two major powers are at odds with each other, with no channel available to deal with and lessen the tensions. The Successor might attempt to repair the break, but he's got enough problems of his own just staying alive within the business. He's a referee without uniform, authority, confidence, or rule book — and his whistle just irritates everybody.

We could ask "who's right?" What we'd find in this, as in most conflicts, is that everyone thinks "I am."

There is no "right," in fact. There are only points of view and, with luck, a shared objective: continuity of a successful business, managed by a family that is able to get along.

But this takes understanding — and acceptance. And how much of that is there in the typical family company? Not much.

Take the issue of work, for example. A fundamental value that's widely accepted in the business world — particularly in the world of business ownership — is the value of hard work. It's common for business founders, especially, to believe the only way to be successful is to work harder and longer than anyone else.

This basic value is generally built into the fabric of every business owning family. It's reinforced by the experiences most business owners have building their businesses. They're familiar with long hours, large risks, uncertainties, anxieties, and crises. That, to them, is a price that's paid for success.

But, suspending for the moment any judgment whether this attitude is proper and justified, it's worth asking whether this culture is readily shared by the successor's wife, The Boss's Daughter-in-law.

It can be, of course, particularly if she grew up in the same kind of environment. But even if she comes from a business owning family, there's no guarantee that she assimilated the culture in which she grew up. Many young men and women today believe in the value of hard work, and they don't really believe lunch comes free, but they also see the negative side of hard work and success. What they see — and want desperately to avoid becoming — are successful people who are leading relatively empty lives.

The successor's wife is likely to appreciate the need for commitment to the business, but she's also likely to defend with great determination, the depth and quality of her personal life. She wants — and will eventually demand — the freedom to define along with her husband what's best for them and their family.

This can cause Dad some severe problems. He knows that she doesn't understand, that she's young, naive, and surely unrealistic. He feels she has little concept of what a gift the business represents. He tries to make her understand. She doesn't want to be made to understand. And so they clash.

This isn't a matter of right or wrong. It's not a matter of facts or evidence. It's a matter of opinion, culture, and personal values, and there's room within every family business for many different people, value systems, and lifestyles.

REPLACING DISAGREEMENT WITH ACCEPTANCE

Once we understand the different worlds people inhabit, it's easier to understand why it's so difficult for people to agree with each other. We could even say that the variations among people are so vast that *agreement* is probably impossible.

Given that, it's better to work toward acceptance, in the

hope that understanding might eventually follow. But if it doesn't, the mere fact that we've been able to accept the other people in the family as well-meaning human beings following their own personal compasses makes it much easier to talk to them. Such acceptance can serve very well to repair that parted communication cable.

The trouble is, of course, that most of us have a tough time accepting the possibility that a situation might be viewed in other valid ways — other than our own, that is. We recognize people are different. That's easy. What's tough is accepting those differences as reasonable and believing in the validity of the opinions arising from those differences.

Business owners have no corner on the intolerance market. They just have the power to be more direct in their prejudices. There's nothing to be gained in placing blame for the disagreements between The Boss and his younger in-laws. What's needed is cease fire and solution — and everybody has a part in that.

The Boss and his spouse should give serious thought to the price they may have to pay for continued insistence on their point of view. It's worth remembering that their children-in-law are much more than chance interlopers. They are powers to be reckoned with, real powers, because the future of the business depends on them, and, of course, they have a significant role in the development of the grandchildren, the next-to-next generation of managers.

Can they accept their children-in-law — and their attitudes — as a given?

On Dad's part, there's a need for recognizing that his Daughter-in-law's motivations stem primarily from love and concern for her family (which, by the way, includes *his* son and *his* grandchildren). She wants economic security, sure. Who doesn't? But mostly she hopes that her spouse can use his talents and abilities to be fulfilled in his work. She hopes, too, that he doesn't have to walk forever in the shadow or under the thumb of his father. She knows this is good for nobody, and Dad, in his wisdom, should know it, too.

For her part, the Daughter-in-law had better realize that this business is, in fact, Dad's. Sure, he says he wants to share it, but the timetable is his to set. Sure her husband has ability, but there's a lot to learn. Of course, he must have responsibility if he's going to learn, but the cost of his mistakes will largely be borne by his father. Just as daughters-in-law aren't born greedy and aggressive, business owners aren't born stubborn and patronizing.

. The Daughter-in-law is going to have to give thought to the reality of her position. She did, in fact, marry into a family business. Business ownership carries with it all sorts of demands and sacrifices, but there are also many benefits which she tends, too often, to overlook — benefits like a growing investment, business opportunity for her children, a chance at autonomy for her spouse.

There are a lot of potential benefits to taking an objective look at the whole picture, and making an honest evaluation of how the benefits and sacrifices balance each other. She has to realize, too, that other members of the family have different values and goals. Their priorities aren't necessarily hers. Can she accept that?

The Son-in-law needs to think about all this, but also his position as guardian of Dad's daughter. Dad's not suddenly going to stop caring about his "little girl," and his standards for her husband's behavior aren't about to change. They're rooted too deeply in love. These are facts.

If the son-in-law doesn't work in the business, he'll have to learn to understand the gifts coming from his father-in-law and try to accept them as gracefully as possible. If he does work in the business, he's going to have to understand that his relationship to Dad is generally a combination of acquiror *and* son. He has the burdens of relationship without many of the advantages of the blood tie.

The Daughter-in-law's husband, the son and heir, needs some education and wisdom, too. Too often he makes the error of deciding the best course is to ease her mind by keeping her uninformed (how can she worry about what she doesn't know?).

It seldom, if ever, occurs to him that this will only make her worry more — about the terrible unknown. She's a partner and rates her share of understanding and responsibility.

It's generally a mistake for a successor to attempt to play mediator between Dad and his Daughter-in-law. The successor doesn't usually see himself in this role, but that's often the effect his behavior has. He practices amateur "diplomacy" (dishonesty by omission) with his Dad and his spouse, succumbing to the powerful temptation to try to pour pacifying oil on his family business waters in hopes that he can smooth over disagreements. But it's a costly sin. His influence is precious and limited. If he uses it wrongly, no matter how much "oil" he uses, it won't calm the storm. The rough water will only return.

His job, as a successor, is not to get his father and his spouse to agree with each other. That's up to chance, circumstance, and *them*. While his best interest lies in their accurate understanding of each other's concerns, the real solution to everybody's problems is going to be his success at qualifying as a successor.

His energy should be concentrated on developing his ability to run a growing, profitable business. His wife's concerns should be given the respect and consideration they deserve. They should be discussed and addressed.

As in Einstein's revised Universe, in the family business there is no privileged observer. Observations are relative to the beholder, and realizing this can serve very well to repair that severed communication line between The Boss and his "second in command" — not to mention opening some of the closed channels between others in the family.

Section II

THE PROBLEMS

Chapter 4
MOTIVATING THE FAMILY
"Why Do Nice People Get Involved with Family Companies?"

Curiouser and Curiouser!
Lewis Carroll

A simple question . . .

. . . With an answer more complex than most of us —
inside or outside of family businesses — realize.

For most people, the answer is assumed — why, it's a
great opportunity and investment, right? (Suprisingly enough,
quality of investment is an answer seldom given by anybody.)

For others, it's a flip, facile "why not?" (which is no answer at all).

As for me, I ignored the question for many years, assuming that the reasons behind my bias in favor of family business
continuity were just below the surface and could be dragged up
whenever I really needed them. Mostly I just assumed.

Then, one winter afternoon at the Cleveland Airport I
was having lunch with Dr. John Ward of Loyola University. I'd
just gone through a particularly wrenching and immensely dis-
appointing "succession" problem of my own and, quite natu-

rally, our conversation turned to explanations and justifications. Within seconds and almost simultaneously, the same question occurred to both of us:

Why, we wondered, do nice people get involved and stay involved with family companies?

We were both professionals with a lot of experience working with family companies. We had seen more pain, frustration, and conflict within family businesses than most people had. We knew first hand how agonizing some of the emotional conflicts could be. We'd both experienced them, first hand. Yet we knew many people who were sticking to their chosen course.

Further, we believed they were right in having chosen that course. We both also believed that they could, in fact, reach their objective successfully.

The unpleasant aspects of business ownership are realities that aren't about to change. We both knew that. A family company represents the supreme management challenge, and the attractiveness of alternative investments (cash, security, liquidity, etc.) often seems proportionately greater. Yet business ownership maintains a powerful, almost magnetic hold over people. It's like marrying young — the horrendous odds against long-term success, and the attractiveness of the alternative single life, seem to have very little power to discourage people from trying.

Surprisingly (to us at least), the exploration hadn't been done. Most articles and theories, most family business "models," were concerned with the "how" of succession and continuity planning. While there's nothing wrong with answering the question "how?" (after all, that's the basic intent of this book), technique isn't enough. We really have to understand why we even bother.

To paraphrase Socrates, an unexamined goal is not worth pursuing.

DO WE USE THE RIGHT "WHYS?"

It would be very difficult for anyone — anyone who's familiar with family business, at least — to deny that the perpetuation of a successful family-owned company is one of the most complicated, frustrating, and difficult tasks human being can take on.

Even at its best, life in a family company is not without stress. There seems always to be some discomfort. A successful company invariably puts pressure on a family. It amplifies the normal frustrations of family life, while it demands so much more from the participants.

Discomfort seems never to be totally absent, even if it's only the "soreness" caused by being forced to run hard. Yet the problem is not so much the pain or discomfort as it is the tendency men and women in family companies have to skirt the true issues and avoid the important questions.

Still, families attempt working together by the hundreds of thousands every year. Millions of people are going through the preliminaries (or post-mortems in too many cases) every day. And, even more remarkable, many of these erstwhile heroes actually *succeed.*

Family companies do perpetuate, generation to generation, and they do so only because the people within the owning families have the commitment, the guts, and the energy to stick the process out. But that still leaves us with the central question: *Why* does it work for some but not for all?

It's relatively easy to come up with a list of pseudo-reasons for sticking it out in the family business pressure cooker. Often, one or more of these function as the driving force behind the process — at least for the individual who "owns" the particular reason. But because these rationales tend so often to be inadequate, poorly thought through, and without roots in the true worth of the family company, they almost inevitably fail their bearers — and just at the time when they need them the most.

I attempt to explore people's reasons for sticking it out every chance I get — individually, in professional relationships with clients, and during family business seminars. I've compared experiences with other professionals in the field. A very remarkable fact continues to emerge from all of this — very few members of families in business use the justification that the business is a good financial investment.

This isn't to imply family businesses are bad investments, but it does indicate a *relative* lack of concern for return on investment compared to all the other reasons people decide to stay in business together. In fact, the family business is more typically seen as an illiquid investment with very little mobility.

So why do they stay?

The reasons seem to be as complex and variable as are human beings themselves. In some cases, the justifications are conscious. In most cases, they're thought about for the first time when the question is asked. Most people seem to simply go through day after uncomfortable day, vaguely feeling, at best, that something isn't right or, at worst, in great emotional pain. Or, conversely, those who are happy and fulfilled by working in their family companies seldom stop to consider why their companies work.

If a journalist were to interview the members of a typical family business, he would hear as many different answers to his basic question ("Why is a nice person like you in a situation like this?") as there were people he interviewed:

THE "WHYS" DAD AND MOM TEND TO USE

INTERVIEWER: *You look tired, disappointed and even driven to distraction, sir. Why do you keep it up? You look like you have enough laid aside.*

THE BOSS: That's a good question. I guess I'm doing it for my family, particularly the kids. It's sort of my legacy to them, a gift of my work and sweat over the years. If it wasn't for the kids, I suppose I would've sold out years ago. It's probably not worth the hassle otherwise.

I: *Things have really been that rough?*

TB: Sure. We've gone through a couple of really tough years, years when markets were drying up and competition was getting more fierce by the day. Frankly, I'm a little tired of it — very tired, in fact. If I wasn't needed to hold it all together until the kids are ready, I'd be sitting in my Bass Boat up at Clear

Lake, retired and taking it easy.

I: *But what about you? Aren't you getting anything out of the business, or out of working? Isn't there something about the business that's keeping you going?*

TB: Oh, I still enjoy some parts of it. But that's not the point. The business is going to be theirs someday, and what they need is me out of their way. They already have some stock, and each of them is going to get a quarter of the whole pie after I'm gone. I feel I have to protect that for them.

I: *What about you, Mrs. Business Owner? Why do you stay involved with the business?*

MOM: Mainly, I stick with it because my husband does. This business is something he always wanted. He built it with his bare hands, and I've always supported him. Now, I feel we have to support the kids.

I: *Was the family business good for your family?*

M: I'm not sure anymore. In the beginning, I would've said yes, no question. Now, things are a lot different with the kids actually working in the business. There do seem to be a lot more fights than before, especially between our son and daughter who work with Dad and their brother and sister who don't. And now that our son-in-law came with us, it's getting even more complicated. Still, I can see everybody's point of view, and everybody deserves a chance.

I: *Well, maybe all those problems mean your family should really get out of the business and do something else.*

M: No. I want to hold the business together so that all our children can have the opportunity their father and I built for them, not just the two who are working. That's what a family is for — and that's why we all have to learn to get along better than we do — and why we have to hold this business together.

THE "WHYS" USED BY SUCCESSORS AND THEIR SPOUSES

I: *Your parents tell me they're sticking with the business so it can be yours someday. Why are you still involved?*

THE WORKING SON: Because I know they're doing

it for me, I guess. That's not an easy thing — knowing that, I mean.

Sure it's tough. I've been working for Dad for 10 years now, and it never gets any easier. Nor do the solutions seem any closer. But it would be stupid for me to change now, after all that emotional investment. And, besides, I've learned a lot about this industry. If I changed companies now, I'd lose all that experience and have to start over.

I: *But what about the early years, when you were still flexible enough to move if you wanted to?*

TWS: Truth is, I never was all that flexible. That's something my wife never understood. First of all, I simply couldn't have made this kind of money on the outside. I didn't have any experience. And, besides, there are a lot of other things to think about over and above my career.

I: *Such as?*

TWS: The rest of my family, for one thing. My brother and sister who aren't working here. Someone has to keep it going for them. And then there's Mom and Dad. It would kill them if this business folded up or were sold to some stranger.

I: *But do these reasons justify the effort you're putting in?*

TWS: I don't think that's the point right now. Eventually Dad'll decide to let go and when that happens — when I'm president — there'll be a lot of time to reap the rewards of my investment. Meanwhile, I'm learning how to become an entrepreneur in my own right.

I: *What about you, The Boss's daughter-in-law. You don't have the same ties to the business or the family as your husband does. Why are you still agreeing to your husband's involvement?*

THE WORKING SON'S SPOUSE: I'm doing it because my husband wants to stick with it. As far as I can see, though, his father doesn't appreciate him, never gives him any credit or responsibility, and is never going to pass along the business.

I: *But what if your husband simply asked you what to do?*

TWSS: If it were up to me (and if we could afford it), we'd quit tomorrow and do something else. It's just not up to me, that's all.

I: *What about you, The Boss's daughter-successor? You're working with your dad, your brother, and your brother-in-law. Why?*

THE WORKING DAUGHTER: Because the business is important to the family. It always has been. That's mainly why I'm here. I had a perfectly good career as an attorney for five years before I came in, but I could see that the business was in trouble.

My husband thinks I'm crazy. He says I could be making more money and enjoying myself more with the law firm, and maybe he's right. But he doesn't understand how important this company is to my family. I couldn't just stand by and watch it go under.

I: *You're her husband. Is that enough reason for you?*

THE WORKING DAUGHTER'S SPOUSE: It's what my wife wants to do, although, God knows, I don't understand it. I mean, what's a competent attorney doing selling machinery?

I'm going along with it because there's a lot of money involved and I figure she's protecting her investment (and maybe her mother's). And, boy, does it need protecting. I don't have a lot of faith in that market. I don't think her brother knows what he's doing, no matter how much Dad wants him to be president, and I think her father's management ideas are somewhere back in Theory A.

I: *But doesn't that make the family company a shaky investment in your mind?*

TWDS: Sure, but who knows, it might work out — and if it does, you can never tell. I might get a job with the company, too.

THE "WHYS" USED BY NON-INVOLVED HEIRS AND THEIR SPOUSES

I: *You're a non-working heir, but your husband is working for your father. That seems like a difficult road. Why do it?*

THE NON-INVOLVED SISTER: I don't know that much about the business, but I do feel it's a great opportunity for our children. That's why my husband is working for Dad, kind of to keep an eye on things and make sure our rights are protected. Dad asked him to come in when he was looking for a job, and I guess we feel some gratitude for that, too.

I: *So your husband hasn't had any problems.*

TNS: Oh, don't get the wrong idea. My husband's had some problems with my brother and sister, and Dad seems to assume my brother will be the next president, but I think in a few years my husband will prove himself equal to those two, even though they've been in longer.

I: *But there's a good chance he won't. What happens then?*

TNS: We'll stick to it because we have as much right to benefit from the business as my brother and sister. It shouldn't make any difference that I want to stay home with our children.

I: *Do you agree with your wife?*

THE WORKING SON-IN-LAW: I think so. Maybe I should've stuck to pharmacology, but I could see that things were getting out of hand in the business and that our kids stood a chance of being cut out of their inheritance.

As far as I'm concerned, my wife has a right to stay home and raise the kids if she wants to, and that decision is no reason why she shouldn't have a say in what happens. After all, she's an owner, just like her brother and sister.

I: *But there's a lot of difference?*

TWSIL: You bet. They were taking salaries out and we couldn't. It just wasn't fair. That's why I'm working in this company.

I: *What about you two?*

THE NON-INVOLVED BROTHER: My brother was trying just the other day to talk me into selling my shares to him when Dad dies. I mean, I thought that was cold-blooded as hell.

Besides, does he think I'm stupid? I can see the company growing. Maybe it doesn't pay dividends and I'm not getting anything out of my shares now, but I know that later on that company is going to represent a significant chunk of change. I'm holding on for that day.

THE NON-INVOLVED BROTHER'S SPOUSE: Someday that business is going to be worth a lot of money — assuming my in-laws don't screw it up beforehand.

I agree with my husband, we have a right to our share.

10 TYPICAL "WHYS" — AND WHY THEY AREN'T ENOUGH

These fictional people represent a composite family business, a typical grouping of relatives and relationships all circling a successful company like moons around a planet. There are many permutations and combinations possible, of course, but the *attitudes* they've expressed represent a valid cross section of rationales for sticking with a family company in transition.

The most striking fact is the almost complete lack of general enthusiasm, the sense of fun that was probably typical of Dad when he was building the company. It's the most telling symptom of a poorly answered family business "Why?". These people remain "in" their family company not so much by choice as by the feeling that they, somehow, should.

But just how well do the typical rationales stand up to hard scrutiny?

RATIONALE #1: *"If It Wasn't for the Kids."*

While there's little doubt that human beings regularly and naturally make sacrifices for their offspring, altruism isn't the only drive determining human behavior. Founders start family businesses for a lot of reasons that have nothing to do with their children — unemployment, ambition, overconfidence, brilliance, marketplace demands — and they stick with those businesses for more reasons than legacy-building (see the discussion of retirement, or more particularly, "semi-retirement" in Chapter 6).

If Dad were solely interested in the future of his children, he would do everything possible to plan the business future and staff the management team to ensure stability and growth. His energy would be directed at training his successors, rigorously and thoroughly, to make sure of their ability to grasp the baton he's offering and carry on the race.

He does some of this, of course, but far from everything possible. He's too busy doing other things, such as enjoying himself, basking in the glory of his hard-earned success, taking advantage of his power and authority, maintaining his own security, and (more important, perhaps, than everything else) making sure he has something to do with himself.

In some senses, he may be doing what he's doing to be *with* the kids. He probably feels some guilt for not spending enough time with them when they were very young and leaving the whole thing to Mom while he built the business. Now, much later, the business can provide him a chance to spend time with the kids without sacrificing his attention to the company.

No. Dad's not doing it all for the kids' benefit.

Nor should he be.

RATIONALE #2: *"Everybody Deserves a Chance at the Benefits."*

Partially, this is a "salaries and perks" justification for family business continuity. Part of it involves the legacy concept — why else did we build this company, if not to use it as a source of benefit for all of us? A larger part of it, though, (and subconscious in most cases) is the fact that these benefits are very easy to get used to — the club memberships, the "business" meetings in exotic locations, the social status, the condo at Vail. Comfort can anaesthetize a whole range of pain, so well, in fact, that it's all too easy to forget the source or importance of the dull ache that's left.

Other, more substantial, benefits are mentioned, too. There's the opportunity to work for yourself, the opportunity to control your own destiny, and the opportunity to maintain relative employment security. For successors, of course, these "opportunity benefits" are carrots rather than rewards — they only come when and after Dad lets go of the helm.

While it seems a poor justification to undergo all of the sweat and trauma of management transition just to make sure our offspring can enjoy a perpetual benefits catalog, the "opportunity benefits" do seem to hold some water. Still, control and freedom are future benefits; they don't explain why so many heirs stay with their family companies waiting for those benefits to accrue.

RATIONALE #3: *"It's the Best Opportunity Available."*

If this statement is true, we can only give that particular business our blessing. Too often, however, this isn't really what's being said. Too often, the family business is the *only,* not necessarily the *best,* opportunity available.

The sentiment can be expressed in a number of ways. We've heard heirs speak openly of their family companies as "safe harbors," and admit they felt that what they knew was preferable to what they didn't know.

These are the statements of prisoners, someone locked in place because of a lack of options. The bars don't have to be obvious. One can be as easily imprisoned by inertia, the love of security, or comfort as by the "hardware" of family business imprisonment: golden handcuffs, lack of outside experience, inadequate training, advanced age. However the doors are locked, it makes little sense for the prisoner to concentrate on adding strength to the bars because they're the only ones he has.

A benign family business will expand the range of options available, not eliminate the need for options. Little happiness can be found in "being kept," and the situation plays havoc with self-respect.

RATIONALE #4: *"There's Too Much Time (Money) Invested To Quit Now."*

The corollary to this can be stated very simply: "Hold on. It'll All Work Out."

While we can have a lot of respect for faith and unremitting hope, few problems in the family business respond positively to the simple passage of time. Without positive, active, well-reasoned approaches to solving transition problems, the situation is almost guaranteed to get worse with time.

Instead of soothing the pain and tribulation, unalloyed hope only guarantees it will all get worse.

RATIONALE #5: *"It's What My Spouse Wants."*

By its nature, a family business is a family affair. It's more than simply a career for the family managers. It's also a "career" for their spouses and their children, a presence that pervades most waking activities, a lot of dreams, and far too many nightmares.

Both spouses "gotta wanna." To defer cherished personal goals on something this important is to remove crucial support from the spouse deferred to. "Do what you think best," all too readily evolves into "Do what you want, but don't expect me to believe in it (or like it)."

RATIONALE #6: *"It's Important to the Family."*

This rationale takes many forms. Here are just a few of the possibilities:

* Dad just couldn't make it without me.

* My sister, or my brother, or Mom (etc.) need me to manage the company and keep the investment safe.

* It would really hurt my brother (father, etc.) if I left.

What's important to the family is to be able to stay together in love, trust, and respect. As long as the business helps this to happen, continuity of the business is important to the family. If, on the other hand, the business is becoming a source of dislike, distrust, and disrespect, fighting to keep it for the sake of the family is to fight for the right to commit "familicide."

A family business serves better as a means than it can ever serve as an end in itself.

RATIONALE #7: *"It's Something Dad Always Wanted."*

This we hear expressed in various ways. "This is what Dad wanted for us." "Dad would have expected us to stay." However it's stated, it expresses a sense of "capture." The burden of guilt and responsibility was placed on the heirs' shoulders by the previous generation, and the heirs reluctantly accede.

Well, Dad might have wanted the family to work together in a successful growing company that he built. He might still want that today. But other questions need to be asked. Is this what is going to happen if the family stays in the business? Will the family, indeed, be able to work *together?*

Parents readily deny these motives, openly stating that

to join the business because "Mom and Dad want it" is definitely the wrong reason for coming into the company. Our statistics are unofficial, but far fewer parents seem to want to force their kids into the business than the "captured" heirs seem to think.

Rather than serving as a justification, this rationale is more appropriately viewed as a side benefit of family business when it's held together for other reasons that are more sound.

RATIONALE #8: *"There's Always the Chance It'll Be Worth More Someday."*

And there's always the chance that it won't.

A successful, growing family business can be an excellent investment, but generally only for working family managers. Minority ownership by non-involved shareholders is a notoriously lousy investment, even if the company is growing and successful. The stock is illiquid, pays few if any dividends, and there's no market for it. Is this the kind of investment that would justify the level of emotional trauma it often involves?

Even for the working owners, who have more opportunity to benefit from their ownership through salaries, perquisites, and the like, the cash portion of their return can often be lower than prevailing rates from other investments. Business ownership offers intangible returns — personal control, fun, challenge, opportunity — which must be figured into total return. If those intangibles aren't there, if the business isn't fun and the family isn't getting along, overall return can be very low indeed.

To stick with it for some undefined, possible future return when today's return is inadequate is to ignore reality and believe, instead, in Shangri-La.

RATIONALE #9: *"We've Got To Protect Our Rights — and the Rights of Our Kids."*

Rights? To what? Not to asset value — the business belongs to the present owners and they can do what they wish with what they own. There are no moral "rights" to an inheritance.

To jobs and salaries? To have it all? To have as much as everybody else? These aren't "rights." They're possibilities, opportunities, gifts — all of which are matters of good fortune, hard work, and commitment that can easily be destroyed by unjustified demands.

This isn't a reason for sticking it out in a family company. It's a cause of conflict and the eventual destruction of everything good and true within that company.

RATIONALE #10: *It's a Great Opportunity To Become an Entrepreneur in Your Own Right.*

I saved discussion of this reason until last because, while it's the most "obvious," it's also the most insidious.

A family company, in fact, is not the best place to develop and express personal entrepreneurship. Oh, it was for Dad, the founder, but he wasn't really building a "family" company. He was just building a company — and he was (in most cases) all by himself. The entrepreneurial venture becomes a family company only with the addition of heirs (in most cases more than one).

While we don't yet have research evidence for this, experience with clients and family businesses in general seems to tell us that personal desire for entrepreneurial freedom is associated very closely with resentment of siblings in the business, and the inability to accommodate the ideas of others.

In short, a second-, third-, or subsequent generation family company is not necessarily the haven for entrepreneurship many heirs seem to expect — at least not the individualistic, heroic, solitary All-American Entrepreneurship so romanticized in our business press.

HOW THE "WHYS" CAN EFFECT THE "HOWS"

While we can criticize many of these relatively negative justifications for accepting the challenge of business continuity, there's little question that they are operative reasons for many people. But, at base, these negative rationales generally underlie many of the frustrations and conflicts that occur in family companies. Perhaps by studying family companies in which harmony, agreement, and respect seem to operate — the "fun" companies, whose owners enjoy working together every day — we could learn what justifications seem to work.

By now it's fairly clear that family companies are not primarily held together because of their qualities as investments. This factor is, and always will be, important, but it seldom seems paramount in the minds of family business owners. Something else, more powerful and persuasive, seems to operate in the best of family companies.

The most positive reasons given for staying together in a family business usually involve its potential for accentuating the positive aspects of family life. This is what holds people together in family companies, despite the tendency success has to amplify the negatives. Members of the older and younger generation alike have said they believe the family business can provide an opportunity to work together, to share mutual interests, and to communicate as professionals.

This is the fundamental "why," at least the one that operates in the most successful families in business. And if we can accept the validity of family togetherness as a reason to stay in business together, then we must also accept the challenge to manage that business and the family in a way that will ensure "togetherness" is achieved.

The negative aspects of the family business should never be accepted as inevitable, unavoidable, and incurable. Once and if they are, we contradict the basic reason for staying involved.

For successful families, the family business helps solve family problems — and keeps them solved. Keeping the business in the family is a way to develop closeness and openness in communication, even though it might not have existed previously in the family. Many successful families find that the business, once the reason why parents and children saw so little of each other, now provides a catalyst for seeing each other more.

In successful families, the family company is like a lens for focusing the shared dreams and values of the family members. The family company is a vehicle for unleashing the power of shared dreams. It allows loyalty, trust, and love to operate in a business environment.

These are the positive reasons for staying together as a family in business, not in theory, but in fact. Most, if not all of these benefits are experienced and expressed in successful family companies — those that have been successful at integrating generations in the pursuit of continuity and success.

HOW "WHY" IS DIFFERENT FOR NON-FAMILY MANAGERS

Often, the family company is much more than simply a family matter. When some or all of the ownership is slated for outsiders, there are some important considerations that have to be made. In these situations, as the above discussion implies, an entirely different set of rationales tend to apply.

In companies with non-family successors, quality of investment is very likely to be paramount for both the present and the future owner. And similar motivations are likely to apply to other non-family managers, who aren't and never were slated for ownership. The likelihood of shared dreams and values, while non-zero, is very low in these cases. Certainly, where dreams and values *are* shared, the owners, the non-family successor(s), and the non-family managers have an advantage. But it's dangerous to assume that these shared values are enough to ensure that the process will be stuck with to the end.

The Boss and his non-family managers should at least discuss the issues, and settle, openly and frankly, their "whys" as early as possible in their relationship. Bitter experience has underlined, many times, the importance of reaching this understanding.

The "whys" are important — for everybody involved in a family company. They determine how the company is managed. They determine the goals that are set. And they set the tone, the atmosphere under which everybody operates.

At bottom, the goal of succession planning in a successful family company is setting up an organization that can help family members as well as non-family managers achieve the positive benefits of business ownership.

So, first, we have to understand *why.* With this done, we're more ready to go on to the "hows," which are the subject of the following chapters.

Chapter 5
QUALIFYING THE SUCCESSORS
"They're Just Not Ready Yet!"

*Any one can hold the helm when
the sea is calm.*
Publilius Syrus

An employment ad written to attract family business successors would probably read something like this:

ENTREPRENEURIAL ASSISTANT

Wanted: *energetic, committed young man or woman for undefined entry-level growth position in a successful family company. Unlimited career opportunity without the restriction of a defined career ladder. No prior job experience required. Indefinite training period will involve observation of all phases of operations without responsibility or authority. Applicant must be patient self-starter with self-confidence, but enough humility to accept continuing suggestions for improvement. Kin relationship to owner is preferred*

*and will be widely known by other employ-
ees, as well as customers, suppliers, and the
general public. All qualified applicants accepted independent of talent or capability.
Salary has no relationship to performance,
and siblings will be paid equivalently, irre-
spective of seniority, experience, or ability.
Spouses acceptable, but discouraged. Apply
in person.*

Well, it *is* a chance, after all. If you read the ad closely,
it seems to imply there's not really a job being advertised, only
a position, but, heck, any talented and intelligent heir should
be able to carve out his or her own job. The business needs a
lot of things — look how much better it should be doing. Wait'll
I grab the ball and run.

Being creative and ambitious, most would-be successors
absolutely refuse to let reality get in their way. So they answer
the ad, apply in person, with the intention of making their own
job, a new and unprecedented job, within Dad's business. But
precisely because what the heir does is unprecedented, he's almost by definition closed off from any job that's connected to
what the company really does.

This alienation often manifests itself in concentration on
strategic planning, computerizing the business, or writing policies and procedures. Nobody else is doing these things, so the
successor naturally does them.

At first glance, this looks fine. After all, these activities
are needed in most family companies. But the effect is far from
ideal.

HOW SUCCESSORS MISS THE ENTREPRENEURIAL "POINT"

Alienation from core activities of the company has interesting effects on the successors involved. I remember a conversation I had one afternoon with the son of an about-to-retire
business owner. This young man was to be named president
later in the year, just before his parents left for a trip to Australia.

When I asked him if the prospect made him nervous, he admitted it did, but he had no doubt he could handle the job. He showed me a copy of his business plan, a monumental piece of work that took up three gigantic binders, and explained where he was planning to take the company.

This family business, which had sales revenues of about $2 million the previous year, manufactured movements for small electronic meters and, like most manufacturing companies during that period, had just gone through one of the worst sales years in its history. The trick, he explained to me, was to find a new sales manager who could fill the void his Dad would leave on retirement so he, himself, could concentrate on carrying out the plan.

Are you going to service your Dad's present customers, I asked?

No, he answered. *I'm going to leave that to our new sales manager. I hate selling.*

Or so he was convinced. He'd never really tried it.

Some months later, another young man approached me after a speech I gave on succession planning. I'd put a lot of emphasis on successor qualification, and he asked if I thought he was qualified to become president of his family company. I asked, in response, what *he* considered his qualifications to be.

He had an MBA, he answered. He was on the boards of two banks, and had designed the entire management information system in his father's company. Right then he was working on computerizing the accounting system and developing a strategic plan for the business.

Do you *think you're qualified,* I asked?

He wasn't sure, he answered.

Is your Dad qualified, I asked?

He thought carefully for a moment, and then nodded.

Selling is Dad's real strength — he could sell anything to anybody. But Dad was a lousy manager. That's why his son had to put together the MIS and redesign the accounting system.

Are you a good salesman, I asked?

Nope. Not my bag. (He'd never really tried it, either.)

Do you think the ability to sell is an important qualification for being president of a closely held business?

For some people, in some businesses, but he was a manager. He could hire people to do that.

He didn't like sales, either.

Both of these successors had gravitated to unfilled management areas, "jobs" that were largely undiscovered within their family companies. In this, they were typical of other heirs in similar situations.

Their initial, and most pressing problem, like most successors', was finding a place in the company — a real place, with real responsibilities, where they could gain real respect. Trouble is, most of the good jobs were filled. Especially those important ones related to the core activities of the company, like sales.

True to their own survival instincts, they made a place for themselves — and for this there's a lot of precedent. In most family companies, filling somebody else's shoes is at once difficult, distasteful, discouraged, and discouraging, primarily because those shoes aren't likely to be empty. Just as it's unusual to find more than one species filling an environmental niche anywhere in nature, we've yet to see two feet in the same shoe.

Successors, consciously or not, imitate nature. Species learned eons ago that it's tough enough fighting predators, without the additional annoyance of fighting neighbors for limited groceries. For efficiency's sake, it's smart to possess an ecological monopoly.

The family business is an ecology — maybe not quite as red in tooth and claw as nature, but just as "exclusive" in niche distribution. Usually, the few existing job slots are filled, and with some fairly fierce competitors. Most packed of all, of course, is the niche filled by the King of Beasts.

There's nothing simple about trying to fit into this seemingly idyllic savannah, even if one comes in as a relative of The King, the way successors do.

The lesser beasts, who've lived with the King for years and who've become highly adapted to their environment, realize the new arrival represents change in their precariously balanced world. It matters little if the successors might not have any interest in displacing existing inhabitants. Suspicion is suspicion, and a perceived threat is a threat.

"You're not one of us."

And things aren't any easier for the would-be successor when he's dealing with The Boss. Successors naturally gravitate toward the throne, because that's where the action is. But that's also where the most massive wall is built.

"All in due time," sayeth The King. *"One does not become the King of Beasts overnight. Go, instead, among the lesser beasts and learn what it is to serve."*

Thus is created that unique environmental limbo inhabited by family business successors. They are forced by circumstances into becoming executive outcasts with no defined place in the local economy. Dad and the old guard cluck and shake their heads sadly over the kid's unfortunate lack of the predatory instinct. Is it a genetic flaw? How could the pup of such a hound dog be little more than a kennel dog?

You have to wonder. Do the genes get diluted over time, with the "predatory" gene mutating into something more soft and spineless? Or is it more likely the heirs are given no significant opportunity to do any real work of their own? Could it be, instead, that they're asked to spend their time in a hopeless attempt to fill holes nobody else even sees?

The choices the successor makes are based on reality.

Closed off from meaningful middle management jobs (if, indeed, there *is* a middle management in the company) and blinded by Dad's blazing presence in the top (typically sales) job, the heirs gravitate toward developing management skills nobody in the company has — usually in the area of planning, accounting, computers, new product development, or personnel.

In this, they're motivated by their education, particularly their graduate education, which tends to concentrate heavily on these professional management skills — the "staff" jobs.

In some companies, this makes sense. The impact heirs can have in staff jobs often *is* a significant and positive one. In few areas of management can this be seen more clearly than in data processing, where business owners' heirs are having major positive impact on family companies as prime movers toward bringing effective computer systems on-line. These results can be seen in other areas, as well. Often the accounting system *could* use remodeling, and there's little question that successful family companies need more professional management in other areas. Moves by successors in these directions are, in most cases, sorely needed.

But is this enough for the successor, the business, and the future?

TWO EXTREMES OF MANAGEMENT STYLE — AND WHY THEY FAIL

Many people believe there are two classes of business manager. In their view, entrepreneurial businesses — the successful ones, at least — are run by entrepreneurs. Whereas major corporations are run by professional managers. The two types of organizations seem to have different needs and the two types of managers seem to have different skills and priorities.

This popular view isn't quite right, however. The world of business and management, like Caesar's great continental battlefield, is divided into three parts, not two. If entrepreneurial ventures and large businesses were all that existed in the economic firmament, we could live very well with a management corps consisting of two ranks: the entrepreneur and the professional manager. But there's a vast middle ground neither of these addresses — the successful entrepreneurial business. The manager who can run one of these is a crucial link we can't afford to miss. Major corporations are beginning to see a need for this person and family companies have always had the need. He must be found if a family business is going to recycle itself, generation after generation.

The management of business change and growth really involves three different kinds of activities, each requiring different management talents and skills. For an organization to stay healthy and growing, it must consistently regenerate, building new life cycles upon old, using growth in certain areas to generate the profitable mature businesses that will, in turn, generate the cash to finance the new ventures.

This usually means that three distinct management styles are needed: the risk-taking entrepreneur, the entrepreneurial manager, and the professional manager. The *risk-taking entrepreneur* is a fighter, a starter, a founder. He begins with nothing and builds fast. The *entrepreneurial manager* is a risk-*manager*. He's a strategist, a developer. He begins with something and builds steadily. The *professional manager* is a *caretaker*. He's an investment manager, a protector, a results insurer. The skills and temperament of each are usually exclusive of each other.

In most family companies, The Boss is, by temperament, the risk-taking entrepreneur. Only reluctantly does he get involved in the "professional manager" jobs that need doing. The successor, sensing that reluctance, gravitates toward the administrative specialties at the professional manager end of the spectrum.

But under these conditions, the risk-taker doesn't have the time or energy to take risk, professional management is done by either the unwilling or the inexperienced, and risk *management* is totally missing. The manager we seldom see in successful family companies is the special hybrid manager — the entrepreneurial manager — required to handle the unique challenges facing the growing portions of the business.

Instead, in most successful family companies, we find a very visible and extremely powerful Entrepreneur firmly at the helm. He or she can be a founder, a successor, or an acquiror. The origin of this CEO doesn't matter so much as his or her outlook, which is generally not appropriate for a successful growing company — and *surely* inappropriate for the mature, cash-generating business.

Typically, the Entrepreneur is a hunter who finds his prey more on instinct and intuition than according to a plan. The Entrepreneur sees opportunities the way a circling hawk can pick out a mouse from a thousand feet away. He pounces, makes use of what he finds, and succeeds. He has the equipment and uses it with expertise and grace — even though much of what he does is done by instinct.

This is an imposing set of skills, to be sure. The Entrepreneur is inspiring to watch. He thrives on risk and stress, and seems energized by hard work. All in all, the Entrepreneur is a majestic, rare bird.

But as the world becomes more civilized, as the Entrepreneur's business succeeds and grows, things become a lot more complicated. Investment is needed. Market segments emerge and need to be managed. Cost control becomes important. Above all, cash management becomes more critical than ever.

It's all too easy for a business to grow into oblivion. The expanding market needs to be met with expanded product lines and wider distribution. All of these still requires entrepreneurial instincts, but now tempered with the technical skills of the manager.

Most Entrepreneurs stumble through this period on sheer genius and hard work — genius to maintain the entrepreneurial edge, hard work to make up for the lack of management skill. Soon, however, the Entrepreneur is in completely over his head.

The business and its markets mature, competition intensifies, and the prey become more wary and hard to catch. There are a lot of products and services out there, all diving for the same end-user buck. Investment in that particular market is no longer attractive, so the successful business begins to generate cash. A need arises for new administrative skills that are about as far from entrepreneurship as one can get. Somehow, and not surprisingly, the Old Hawk finds it harder and harder to adapt.

The evidence of the Entrepreneur's fading appropriateness is generally all around. The old bird just can't cover all that's going on. As counterweights to all the scurrying customers on the ground, there are increasing hordes of new competitors in the air, some of them fairly dangerous. He finds it impossible to divide duties, or to let others handle parts of what he's always done himself. Things are changing faster and more furiously day by day and the Entrepreneur is becoming more and more confused by the insufficiency of the old skills.

The pace of competition is intensifying and the market is being divided into smaller and smaller pieces. Mistakes are more difficult to cover up with hard work. Events are taking on a stubborn life of their own and are much less malleable under the strong hands of genius.

The Successor is a good observer. Initially, he wanted to be a hunter just like the Entrepreneur, but that niche is plugged by The Boss's oversized carcass. Watching the Entrepreneur operate from afar, and seeing how he's being overwhelmed by change, the successor comes to the conclusion (a comforting one, since the main pass is blocked anyway) that being an Entrepreneur is not really a Good Thing at all. What's needed is a totally new and different approach.

The heirs and successor-managers, looking in from their system-imposed exile, see what they interpret as Their Chance. If The Boss can't handle the new world, somebody else will have to — and who better than your's truly? Thus, out of an amalgam of loneliness and hope, desperation and ambition, a new kind of manager is born: The "Professional."

The Professional is anything but a hunter. Instead he's an administrator, a gatherer, a husbander of resources. Because of his superior sense of organization, he tends to dismiss the Old Hawk as the atavistic remnant of an earlier, simpler age. He respects him, to be sure. It's hard not to, particularly since the Entrepreneur runs the whole valley, but the Professional knows his time will come. It's just a matter of hard work and patience.

Professionals tend to be opposites of Entrepreneurs ("But I don't like sales!"), which does little to help the already strained relationship between the kid and The Boss. Entrepreneurs believe in action. They respect aggressiveness, direct approaches, swift decisions. Sight the target, lock on, and dive. *That's* the way a real Entrepreneur works. But the Professionals believe in planning. They respect calm deliberation, careful approaches, and considered decisions. Define the targets you're looking for, bracket them carefully before committing, then move in steadily and deliberately. *That's* the way a real Professional works.

This conflict between the old generation and the new isn't very productive. It's not like evolutionary pressure where old difficulties lead to new solutions. In the family company, *both* the Entrepreneur and the Professional are appropriate management styles in their proper places, but those places have to be defined and the managers have to match skills with needs.

The Professional, despite what the successor might think, is not the next stage of owner-manager evolution. It's not necessarily an improvement either if bureaucratic precepts are applied, unadapted, to the growing small company. On the other hand, despite the Entrepreneur's prejudices, "professionalism" is not a genetic defect. It does manifest some significant survival traits and is fully appropriate to the mature business in a mature or declining market.

DEFINING THE ANSWER: THE "ENTREPRENEURIAL" MANAGER

Few family companies with succession problems are new, start up ventures. Neither are they primarily mature businesses in declining markets, although this is far from uncommon. No, most successful family businesses contain within their walls three stages of development: new businesses which are feeding growth businesses, which, in turn, are growing into mature businesses to feed the new ventures. And so should the recycling continue.

With this as a definition of a truly successful family company, we can begin to define the successful manager of such a company. The growing, vital, recycling family company needs:

1) A manager who is careful and deliberate, but who can sense when an opportunity requires quick and risky action.

Smaller companies can't afford to let too many opportunities fly by untouched. They don't have the mass and momentum larger companies have, nor do they have the resources to create opportunity at will. While it's true that rash action is more risky for a successful company with a lot more to lose than a new venture, rashness and risk remain very important components in the success formula.

How do we know? It's obvious, really. The potential competitors will be risk-takers and they have to be fought on their own turf. Significant threats to the family company will almost always come from aggressive competition. After all, that's how the family company got where it is in the first place.

Thus, the managers of a growing, successful family company will have to be managers who can both stay ahead of the increasing complexity of the business, *and* maintain the aggressive entrepreneurial spirit that defined success in the past.

2) A manager who understands the opportunity value of profit.

Successful family companies can become real cash cows. In fact, at just the time when management transition is becoming a genuine concern, the existing business is probably entering or well within the mature portion of its life cycle curve. It's all too tempting, particularly for Entrepreneurs who've gone through the sweaty process of building, to see the generated cash either as a just reward for the energy expended, or a fragile resource that has to be saved and protected at all costs. The trouble here, of course, is that cash cows can't be milked forever, nor can they long stand an accelerating accumulation of cash in retained earnings (the IRS has definite opinions on this).

Professionals, on the other hand, are playing with other people's money. To them, funds are an abstract quantity, tools to pay for organization, resources, and staff, or a commodity to be managed in liquid investments. To a Professional, idle funds are worse than no funds at all, but funds "at risk" are an essentially foreign concept.

The problem with this outlook — for the family company, at least — is that business survival requires a certain amount of internally leveraged risk. The plank is funding, the fulcrum is a stable business, and the pressure on the long end of the plank must come from an aggressive, risk-taking management. The key is that the taste for risk must be balanced against the need to manage the whole leverage system.

To continue growing and maintain success, today's business must take the risk of financing tomorrow's. But the risk must be wisely tempered. If that financing is done at the expense of a healthy balance sheet, or at the expense of the previous generation's security, the price paid may be higher than the business can afford. The Entrepreneurial Manager will understand the conflicting demands on company profits, and manage those profits to ensure both a reasonable return for the present owners and intelligent reinvestment for the owners of the future. If there's no cash investment in the future, there will be no future.

3) A manager who can both understand his or her limitations, and act in spite of them when necessary.

For a new venture, genius is often enough to overcome a whole range of personal weaknesses in the entrepreneur. Since he isn't weighed down by all the baggage a successful company entails, the Entrepreneur can move quickly to minimize weaknesses and overcome mistakes. But the manager of a successful, growing company doesn't have that luxury. He can't run the whole thing alone. He needs the help of people who are strong where he's weak.

The Entrepreneur has difficulty accepting this fact, however. He's learned over the years not to depend on anyone but himself. His self-confidence and self-reliance are what brought him through all the problems and setbacks of his life. How can his weaknesses be of any real concern? He succeeded, didn't he? Yes, but in a different world, with almost no organization and very little to lose. Can he really do it all alone today?

The Professional has the opposite point of view. He's a team player. Nobody's an island, two heads are better than one, three better than two, and so forth. "Networking," no longer "rugged individualism" has become the cliche, the modern answer to challenge. To his way of thinking, the loner is lost in this modern world. And he's right, there. The loner *is* isolated — and at great risk in an increasingly complex world. But the growing family company, even if it's successful, can't be run by committee. There's not enough momentum for that. It needs leadership and it continues to need that entrepreneurial spark and insight that will keep it ahead of the active competition and quick enough to escape the crushing treads of the larger companies in the industry.

The Entrepreneurial Manager, therefore, is someone who is capable of putting together a working *team* of competent people to back him up and fill in essential skills where necessary. He's able to determine what strengths the company needs, to develop them as far as possible in himself, and then find others to smooth out the low spots.

In short, the Entrepreneurial Manager can — and does — ask for help. But not always. Any team he creates will also need strong, inspired leadership. A network or committee isn't enough for the small, growing company. This Hybrid manager is also going to have to swallow humility, ignore doubts and confusions, make decisions, and give direction.

4) A manager who understands how to balance action with planning — and vice versa.

Entrepreneurs, almost by definition, are *doers*. Action is their strong suit. They have an almost irresistible drive to control their environment and make it malleable to their will. Their experience and their inclinations convince them the way to handle a problem is to wade into it, swinging. There will be some wasted effort. Some possibilities will be destroyed, but ultimately he who acts will win out — *because most other people don't act.*

Professional managers (at least as we've defined them here) see the entrepreneur's action as blind groping, their success as dumb luck. Professionals prefer to think through their actions before taking them. They prefer to build models, draw diagrams, explore options, and predict results. Explore every action on paper or, better yet, in a computer before deciding, they believe. That's the safest — and surest — route to success.

But the Entrepreneurial Manager — the hybrid manager the successor should become — is less opinionated, and he sees both the talents and the limitations of the other two. Blind action is dangerous, he believes. Granted, the Entrepreneur survived his own hyperactivity, but that's because he had so much mobility. He could dance out of his own way. He was small, flexible, able to react quickly. Unfortunately, the successful business is too big for that. It's more cumbersome, and a mistake can cost heavily. But this caution doesn't lead the Entrepreneurial Manager to inactivity. It moves him toward deliberated activity. Think (but not too long) and act (but not too quickly). Moderation in all things, yes, but get all things done.

HOW ENTREPRENEURIAL MANAGERS ARE MEASURED

We've already looked at the need for a "real" job to develop the necessary management skills (Chapter 1), but skill alone isn't enough. Somewhere, too, the successor has to develop the best qualities of the entrepreneur — calm strength, firmness, and the courage to see events by his own light, not the reflected light from adversaries, friends, or loved ones. This is a subtle quality that's only partially developed through responsibility and experience.

The development of a successor into an Entrepreneurial Manager is the result of careful cross breeding and grafting. History, facts, and common sense demonstrate over and over again that whatever success there is in a family company has probably come from the owner-manager. This is true whether the successors like it or not, whether or not they think his management style is out of date, and, yes, whether or not the company is growing *today*. Success and the owner-manager are synonymous, regardless of the state of the art, the reality of recent "megatrends," or the heir's MBA. Unless the next generation is able to come to terms with this, their full development as managers in their family company simply will not take place.

A clever, if not widely remembered Broadway show tune of a few decades back asked: "What can be 'fair' in 'farewell' . . . where is the 'good' in 'goodbye'?" It was a nice play on words, one that suggests another: "Where is the 'success' in 'successor'?" A good question that can be the starting point for understanding this whole problem of fitting into the family company.

Success and succession have to be sold to and negotiated with Dad. And in the absence of actual responsibility as a business owner, the best way to measure how far successor managers have developed toward *entrepreneurs* is to measure how well that sale has been made. This, for the son or daughter of a business owner, is the capstone of personal growth — finding a way to work out a mutually respectful relationship with The Boss and his peers.

The Boss has to be convinced that it's worthwhile to try teaching. He has to be convinced the successor's mind is at least open to "proven" ideas. And he has to learn to respect his student. The most important process in a successor's management development is working out a relationship with The Boss that's etched into the steel of *mutual* respect, *mutual* benefit, *mutual* understanding, and *mutual* agreement. I don't emphasize "mutual" only to improve the meter of my prose. Mutuality is the critical measure of the lasting quality of any relationship forged between The Boss and the successors.

Sure, it requires patience, persistence, even courage. It's worth asking, though, why so many heirs cringe at the prospect of confronting Dad with their own needs and ideas. Could it be a lack of conviction rather than the more obvious fear of failure or rejection. Is it Dad's "no" that they fear, or the possibility he might ask "why?"

Taking refuge in plans and "professionalism" might be comforting, but it isn't going to answer that crucial question. If the successor can't withstand Dad's disagreement, disapproval, or even "stubbornness," he or she is never going to develop the entrepreneurial complements to professionalism: confidence, leadership ability, and aggressiveness.

Often, in the face of rejection and lack of credibility, the successor's reaction is to reject, in return, the values of those he sees as standing in his way. But the future of the company depends on achieving a creative fusion of the old and the new in the coming chief executive, a combination of entrepreneurship and professionalism, of courage and sensitivity, of self-confidence and humility. Again, the "real" job will, of course, go a long way toward building many of these traits in the successors, but even more is needed.

We could ask The Boss to adapt to the changing circumstances around him, and it would be useful if he could do so. But, realistically, that's probably not a fair demand to put on him. It's one thing to evolve a management style at the beginning of your career, and a much different thing to *change* your style after many years of success. The Boss could argue (and, in many ways he would be right) that he's paid his dues and should be able to harvest some of his rewards. He's happy the way he is. It's the next generation's turn to work hard and adapt.

A key lies in how the relationship develops between the owner and the heirs, and the touchstone measure of this relationship is how well or how badly they negotiate the future with each other. Good rapport between Boss and successor has happened. It's been the key to successful transition in most of the family companies who've made it through the process.

What the family company needs in its successor-managers is a creative combination of Entrepreneur and Professional, a hybrid manager capable of professionally managing a growing company while maintaining the entrepreneurial spirit and drive that is its energy source. Developing that kind of manager is a complex job The Boss and the successor have to undertake together, although the successor has the prime responsibility. Evaluating him is a subtle process of measuring his acceptance by The Boss — a process so subtle, that it requires the intervention of outsiders, particularly outsiders who are Dad's peers. How these outsiders get involved, however, is a subject all its own (Chapter 9).

The qualification of heirs is much more than a simple matter of learning technique. There's a subtle wisdom involved with managing a growing business, a wisdom best learned by simultaneously doing and listening — not by increasing specialization in one or the other.

Chapter 6
RETIRING THE BOSS
"He's Back!"

*Habit is habit and not to be flung
out the window by any man, but
coaxed down the stairs a step at
a time.*

Mark Twain

It was a company that seemed to have its succession plan well put together. The successor and I had met during a seminar and kept in touch, on and off, during the following two years. During that time, his father set a retirement date, bought a home in Arizona, and openly announced his departure to customers, suppliers, and employees.

I remember having a relaxed discussion with the young heir a week before the presidency was to be put in his hands. It was a good time for him, and his dad seemed happy. The major problems he foresaw mainly concerned the economy and how he could grow as quickly as he planned.

We corresponded a few times over the following year, and spoke a few times by phone. Everything seemed to be going well . . . until my phone rang shortly before midnight one week-day evening. Groggily, I picked up the receiver, to hear a few seconds of heavy breathing on the other end. The successor's familiar voice quickly dispelled any thoughts about a crank call, but his tone was unusual. I heard a muttered phrase that seemed to groan under it's own emotional pall:

"*He's BACK!*"

And so, indeed, he was. Maybe the Phoenix sun that shone on his Dad's "retirement" home had been too hot. Maybe the fairways got a little too familiar. Or the neighbors weren't very stimulating. The specific cause wasn't all that obvious, but this retired owner-manager had decided, after a year of the "good life," that the real world was back at the office.

And back he came. His son, with reluctance and resignation, settled back to watch the recrowned "Chairman of the Board" begin again to open the mail on Saturday mornings and make his accustomed decisions about acceptable letterhead designs and placement of the office furniture. And that was only the beginning.

What went wrong?

WHY RETIREMENT IS SO DIFFICULT

Many owner-managers have "plans" for their retirement — well, they call them plans, but they're little more than fantasies, self-delusions and daydreams. The typical thought is to get in some golf, or maybe some travel. Others plan to fish a lot or devote themselves to farming that little patch of rocky soil they bought up in Vermont. They "plan," in their various ways, to do all the things they never could find time for while they were building the business.

But they seldom ask themselves just *why* they never found time for these things they "always wanted to do." After all, if these avocations are attractive and interesting enough to be chosen to fill the next 20 years of retirement, why weren't a few hours found for them in the previous 30 or 40? It's hard to avoid a nagging suspicion. Could it be they didn't find the time because they really didn't *want* to take the time?

To carry these musings even further: Maybe, just maybe, most successful business owners simply don't want to quit working.

It may come as a surprise, but most business owners, when pressed for an answer, will frankly admit they never want to retire. The less candid among them don't want to, either, I believe. They just find it difficult to admit, for a number of reasons. One of the least recognized but most widely known facts about (and among) business owners is their desire to stay on the job until the guardian angel collects their Green Stamps. And they know it — maybe they won't *admit* it, but they know. It's obvious by the way they act.

More accurately, it's obvious by the way they fail to act.

Oh, the business owner talks about all the great things he and Mom are going to do someday. You know, the chauffeur driving the van all over the countryside. Or the house in Phoenix or the condo in Ft. Myers. Travel, too. Don't forget travel:

"When I retire, me and the little lady are going to go around the world, to all the places we've never been."

And never really wanted to see?

Too many of us play at retirement. We dream about it in occasional idle moments. We pine for it when we're at our most frustrated. But seldom, if ever, do we actually think about what it entails or make serious plans for it. This failure isn't the unique flaw of successful owner-managers. It's a form of self-hypnosis that seems to affect almost everybody.

This almost universal failure to plan an organized "retirement" can have some awful effects on the retiree, but the complications don't stop there. There are other people involved, and sometimes, as in the owner-manager's case, a family business, too. Retirement can sometimes weigh heavily on the whole crew, a long-awaited windshift that never seems to come. It can almost be *felt* in some family companies — the expectation of and the growing cynicism about Dad's "retirement" can sometimes hang over everything like a palpable emotional smog.

It's not really The Boss's failure to retire that causes the problem (after all, he seldom does more than hint he's going to do it). The real difficulty comes from the fact that everybody else plans their lives around their expectations that he will, in fact, do it.

(Everybody else except Mom, that is. She built her life around his absence and his almost total preoccupation with the business, so his retirement is not so much an expected event, as a feared possibility. When he retires, she will be expected to follow suit — and totally readjust and reorganize a life she already enjoys. But more about this later.)

TYPICAL RETIREMENT "PLANS," AND WHY THEY FAIL

Dad's hints about retirement and his wistful musings about the world's great country clubs occur very seldom, and then only when he's feeling particularly relaxed and avuncular — which is usually less than 10% of the time. To plan around such emanations of occasional good digestion is to ignore all of the more real and more common behaviors the owner-manager demonstrates — the other 90% of the time. In fact, if we interpreted his *behavior* rather than his infrequent hints about his glorious sunset, we'd see that The Boss really doesn't seem to take retirement very seriously at all.

We have other evidence beside his behavior. Consider as an example the viability of a typical retirement "plan" of a typical business owner.

Has anybody, other than maybe an Arnold Palmer, survived, psychologically, 20 years of incessant golf? At 18 holes a day, 85 or 90 strokes a round, seven rounds a week, that's just less than 660,000 golf balls smacked off the end of a shaft over 20 years. I'll leave it as an exercise for the reader to calculate how many casts into the lily pads that same period would mean to the retired entrepreneur-turned-fisherman.

How much can a person stand, before he just goes and climbs his final wall?

If we take the time to look around us and consider the evidence, it would appear that, for most people, in most walks of life, retirement is not a good thing. If nothing else, we at least can conclude that most business owners either avoid it desperately, deteriorate in it, or — as in the case of my friend's homing father — return, inevitably, to the family business like the buzzards to Hinckley, the swallows to Capistrano, and politicians to Washington after Labor Day.

Why? The business owner's thoughts about retirement are generally unrealistic, impractical, naive, illogical, and unworkable. For successors, spouses, employees, suppliers, or advisers to act upon them, or to plan the future of a family or business around them is as sensible as planning a picnic in Buffalo in February on the basis of a weatherman's prediction of 80-degree temperatures. Sure, he should know — but the physical evidence and plain common sense dictate a large dose of caution. The "picnic" isn't likely to happen. In fact, simply trying to get there is likely to result in a lot of wheel-spinning and fishtailing, finishing, in the end, hopelessly stuck or smashed up against a sturdy old oak (and we all know who that gnarled old tree is).

It's difficult, in many ways, for somewhat "younger" folk to understand the problems faced by the preceding generation in fulfilling it's own vague promises to retire. Why is it so tough? They seem really drawn to the idea, and say they've earned it (who can disagree?). It sure seems attractive to be able to rest on the laurels of a productive and fruitful life. That's what we're all after, isn't it — the achievement of success, respect, and an accomplished dream? Most outside observers would be convinced that The Boss's accomplishments would give anybody pride and a sense of satisfaction. How wonderful it would seem to be able to sit back and enjoy those victories.

But is it so wonderful? Does Dad, in fact, get his greatest reward from a terminal pat on the back? Can he retire in peace and joy knowing he's done everything he's going to do?

Not usually, because dreams are never self-limiting. Goals aren't really meant to be reached; they're meant to be *passed*. It might look like goals are ends to outside observers, but within each functioning person's heart is an ever-present drive to do new things.

Just consider what it really means to have "had" a good life. Generally, it means that we have more years behind us than before us. It means that most of the good things are memories, not possessions or expectations. It means that our admiring "public" is admiring us on the basis of what we've done more than on the basis of what we can do. In some senses, having had a good life can be little more cheering than having a well-written epitaph. Both imply that the best part is over.

In reality, The Boss is *having* a good life *now*. Sure the past was good, but that's the past. Today is what counts and today is just fine the way it is. He's not resting on any laurels. He's sampling the fruits of his success, maybe, or taking a few moments out for a little harvesting. But resting? Nope. He's still moving just as fast and hard as ever.

He identifies with the company he built. The company is identified with him. To break with that mutual identification would be to sever the taproot of his personality. That's not a culmination. That's a termination of something that's always been one of the most important things in his life.

Some reward.

But retirement doesn't have to represent a severing from everything meaningful. It could, in fact, represent a move to something new, something with the same kind of potential the company had decades before when The Boss began his career. In a vague sense, this is what Dad wants and needs in retirement. But does he look for it? Does golf have that kind of potential? Fishing? Cribbage?

Possibly for a rare few — but I've yet to meet one of those.

WHY STAYING AT THE HELM IS NO ANSWER

Maybe it's okay that his retirement plans aren't all that firm, Dad might say. So I don't retire. It's my business. What's wrong with remaining active and involved throughout life?

Nothing. But we're not talking in a general sense. We're discussing something very specific: Dad's continuing, active involvement in the family business. That company is a growing, changing organism, and it has needs that are less and less compatible with Dad's as time passes. The problem with aging is that it brings with it two things at once: a lessening desire to get involved in new projects and increasingly limited time in which to accomplish the ones we have.

A growing business generates new ideas. It attracts managers who want to invest energy in those new ideas, directions and projects, and who have the time to make them happen. The Boss has every intention of going along with all this, but as time passes the business future farther and farther outdistances his own narrowing horizon.

For the younger manager, a fresh idea is a new path to be explored. For the older manager, a fresh idea implies that much of what he's learned over the years will have to be questioned — and very likely changed, diminished, or expanded.

Although the older manager has more of the skills of his craft and more power at his fingertips than the younger person following him, he's also carrying a lot more baggage. Packed tightly and all confused in his knapsack of life are his habits, his management style, his basic values of life and work, all demanding that decisions be made a certain way — and all making radical reorganization an almost overwhelming prospect.

It's usually true that The Boss is better than anyone else at what he does best. He reached that position by concentrating on the development of some highly specific skills — to the general exclusion of others. His skills are his major intellectual possessions, and the truths he holds to be self-evident (and there tend to be many of them), he cannot, by definition, question. After all, he is, by definition, the expert.

Is it merely a coincidence that the older we get, the more likely we are to lament the crumbling values of today and feel vague forebodings for the future? It's surely not a function of the times in which we live. Older men and women have been expressing similar sentiments for centuries, probably millennia. No, it's not a coincidence. It's just a reflection of the part of life we really value — the time when we were growing, when our future was still a future, when we were striving and building toward our goals.

"Those were the days," we say more and more often as the years pass. And the more today is different from yesterday, the more those *were* the days — passed, gone, never to be repeated.

We might be tempted to ask "so what?" What has all this to do with retirement?

Well, as people become successful and learn more about the work they're doing, that knowledge often restricts their ability to maneuver. They know too much. They've seen too much. They've done too much. Too much, that is, of what they do best. At first, we tend to approach problems with confidence in the existence of clear cut solutions. Later, as we learn more about those problems, we falter. The problems we know well become gray and interconnected with no clear solutions.

The business owner is no exception to this. As he gets older, he walks along inside an ever narrowing canyon. If he doesn't change direction soon enough and with enough forethought, he finds himself totally closed in by his own experience. He can't go on because his path becomes too narrow to travel. He can't change direction because the walls of his experience press in on him from both sides. And he can't retrace his steps because there simply isn't enough time or energy to go back and begin again. The only answers that seem open to him, then, are (1) "retire" into a vacuum, or (2) to hold in place and struggle against the rabble who are rising and fomenting revolution against the old order.

The first option — retirement into a vacuum — can result, as we've already seen, in a suddenly changed mind ("He's Back!"). It's not really an option. It's more of a temporary delusion that has the same ultimate outcome as option 2.

If, on the other hand, The Boss insists on Option 2, and stays in his job, his restricted flexibility *in his business* can have some severe consequences for that business.

The young have a relative advantage over him — at least with respect to the company. They have the time to get involved and can be profligate with their energy. They're not weighted down by his "baggage," either. They have less idea what "can't be done." They're only beginning their process of setting expertise into concrete.

Creativity, in general, comes easier to those who are mastering a skill than to the man or woman who's the proven master. Sure, the master has within his grasp all of the complexities of his craft, but that very mastery makes it very difficult for him to break away from his past and his training to try something new. That's too much like beginning apprenticeship all over again. The master is committed by the vastness of his experience to the business-as-it-is. The apprentice sees what is, but also has the fresh eye needed to recognize contradictions and inconsistencies, as well as fresh opportunities.

Questioning assumptions, habits, and basic strategies all are the stuff of the future. We don't have to wonder if these are necessary for the business to succeed. We *know* they're necessary because that sort of questioning is precisely what led to The Boss's success as a younger manager, before his awe at what could be done was overwhelmed by the need to protect all the many things he *did*.

All right, neither of his options work. So what's he supposed to do?

My logic to this point seems to have put us on the pointy antlers of a seemingly hopeless dilemma. Most of us don't want to retire, and if we do, we do it without enough forethought to avoid the predictable disappointment. Yet, if we stay with what we do well, we inevitably become less and less adaptable and creative in our skill. Can't retire. Can't stay. Now what?

Quite a lot, actually.

The question of retirement isn't really a dilemma. It's not really a matter of either/or, because there are far more than two options available. The real trick is finding ways to uncover those other possibilities.

To begin with, it would be useful if we all threw the word "retirement" out of our working vocabulary. In its classic meaning, "retirement" implies withdrawing from work, business, public life (and life in general?). We make the mistake of treating it as an option when it's actually more of an unfortunate fate we should try to avoid.

To stop doing is to die — maybe not physically, although

we've all seen sad examples of just such a result — but to keep doing the same thing long past the time the critical edge is lost can be just as destructive. The decision not to "retire" doesn't necessarily imply that we have to stay in our present occupation.

Change is the soil of growth, so it seems self-evident that the chronic resisting of change is an almost certain sign of decline. Change is the stuff of adrenaline and excitement — and an extender of time. Remember the endless summer days of childhood? A repeating newness has a way of slowing down the passage of time and expanding our awareness.

And change needn't be disorienting, not if it's the kind of change we seek. Nor does stability represent real comfort if it's only another way to say "stagnation."

There is an answer to the retirement dilemma — shatter the horns. The alternatives aren't limited only to "keep doing" or "stop doing." *The answer is to do something else* — to find ways we can keep alive the excitement and fun that drew our energy to the skills that made us successful.

This is true for all of us, but it's particularly important for the business owner who has an interest in the continued growth and survival of the business he built. The health of his business and the commitment of his successor-managers depend on his ability to find that acceptable new career. Masters must make way for the journeymen if stagnation of the guild is to be avoided.

Coherent business plans, qualified successors, and agreeing spouses are all important for the future of the family company, but figuring out where Old Dad is going, and where he wants to go in "retirement" is more important. It's important for The Boss's health, the successors' sanity, and the sustained growth of the business. In family companies that have managed transition smoothly, a central success was finding a way for the present owner-manager to become the "former" owner-manager. Those who've done it right have managed to get it done sometime before the "Shame He Waited So Long" threshold was irrevocably crossed.

But — and I can't overemphasize this "but" — just stepping out of the flying airplane so somebody else can have a chance at the controls is no solution for the business owner or anybody else connected with him. He can't really leave unless he has somewhere acceptable to go — and no loyal member of his family would even ask him to walk into an abyss.

COMPONENTS OF A REAL RETIREMENT

Most career "evolutions" that have worked well over time managed, somehow, to fulfill each of the following requirements:

1) Real Retirement solves the retiree's security problems.

A primary reason why many business owners want to hold onto control of their companies is to make sure somebody else doesn't mess up their investment.

"Sure," The Boss says, "I'll get out of the way and let the kids run it — but I want to know everything they're doing and I want the ultimate veto. Everything I have is in that company."

The concern is justified, of course, and if The Boss has no choice but to keep his or her assets tied up in the company, the desire to maintain control would be justified, too. But, in more cases than business owners think, it's not necessary to risk the asset base to achieve management transition. The growth as well as the risk can usually be moved to the shoulders of the young.

This isn't a book about estate planning, but we are concerned with options here. Probably the best few hundred bucks or so The Boss could spend would be to take a good attorney or life underwriter out to lunch and just let him brainstorm about options available for protecting assets while giving the heirs ownership. More than likely, The Boss will be so astounded he'll forget to eat his scampi.

These techniques can take many forms. Just a few examples of approaches:

*RECAPITALIZATION: This is a whole family of methods for reorganizing the kinds of stock issued by the company. Commonly, recaps are done primarily to allow more flexibility in shifting assets from one generation to another. There are many ways to go about this, but the most common approaches usually involve converting common shares into a mixture of voting/non-voting stock, which allows the business owner to place management control wherever he wants it (yes, he can also keep it in his own hands), while equity can be shifted to the next generation.

The present owner, for example, could keep his voting shares and direct their transfer to the successor(s) in his will after the Persistent Reaper has superseded Dad's need for security. The existence of non-voting shares can allow him much more flexibility in distributing equity.

This sort of approach, combined with a gifting program can do a lot to solve the business owner's fear of losing control, but it does have one disadvantage. It keeps management control in the present owner's grip, thus keeping him tied to the operation of the present company. While this may fit The Boss's plans, it's unlikely to fit the long-term plans of the successors.

*SALE OF OPERATING ASSETS: What if The Boss really wants to free himself of concern about the day to day operation of the company so he can pursue his "Renaissance"? What if the successors have more taste for risk than he, and want to *grow*? Using this technique, the business owner can transfer control of the company immediately to his successors, while at the same time protecting his security.

Typically, the successor managers form a new company, to which the old company sells its key operating assets for a long-term note. The real estate and equipment could be made available to the new company through a lease, thus keeping ownership of those assets in the hands of the present owners. Through this approach, the original company is turned into a holding company owning assets and generating cash. The operating risks are transferred to the new company — actually, the successors — accomplishing the major goals of both the present and future owners.

*CREATING A SUBSIDIARY: In cases where the present owner has some major disagreements with the direction the successor managers want to go, he could protect himself, while

giving them their heads, through the establishment of a subsidiary company. The old company invests cash in a subsidiary, getting preferred stock in return. The common stock of the new subsidiary would be owned by the successors, who therefore take the risk and benefit from the growth. The original company is at risk, of course, but that risk is defined and controlled, and limited to the extent of its investment.

The point of these examples is not to *recommend* one or the other of the techniques. The tax and business implications are too complex to be adequately dealt with in this kind of overview. But they should demonstrate, in a small way, the varied options available to achieve ownership transition with controlled and defined risk.

Security needs can be handled with planning and competent professional help. One thing is sure: if they're not handled, The Boss's "retirement" plan has about as much viability as a gnat at a toad convention.

2) Real Retirement absorbs the retiree's creative energies.

A few years ago, I met a business owner and his three sons who'd worked out a neat solution to the retirement question. This owner manager has founded a successful window distributorship in the Midwest. After 15 years of building respected and profitable business, however, he found his becoming stale. It wasn't the fun it used to be, and he was ing more and more of his time administering the com something he disliked (and, predictably, didn't do w

Fortunately (and this wasn't a matter of luck three sons had worked for other, larger distributor est had been a successful salesman for the compa plier. They were competent, ready, and wante running the company. But where would Dad

He'd had that answer in mind for a a convention, he met the inventor/manuf light system who was having a hard tim lights were risky products most dist preferred to avoid (they had an anno

Dad felt this model was right up his alley. He knew the industry. He could sell. He believed in the product. This, he decided, was where he would go.

In a variation on the "growing subsidiary" theme, he gave control of the original company to his sons in exchange for a cash investment in the new skylight company he owned and controlled. Both companies are successful today. In fact, the skylight venture is doing better than the original company, and Old Dad's beginning to face the same administrative headaches he'd experienced with the original company. The odds are good there's a new venture brewing somewhere on the horizon.

Creativity can be absorbed in many ways. They don't all have to be as ambitious as a new venture. I've seen examples of restaurateurs who passed the business over to the kids and spent their time making specialties at tableside, talking with the customers. I've seen business owners who went back into the lab to their first love: developing new products. I've seen new charities founded and funded, or hospitals built and managed. I've seen books written, consulting firms formed, and fallow farmland reclaimed. The key to every one of these new careers, however, was the fun and challenge they represented to the person "retiring." That's why they worked.

3) Real Retirement allows the successor-managers to have their heads.

Just as The Boss has to go somewhere, someone has to be around to fill his old job, bringing with them the required commitment, energy, and talent. If The Boss leaves in theory but not in practice, the message is transmitted that nothing has really changed. And, in fact, nothing really has. The buck still stops in The Boss's lap and nothing's been done except to make the unfortunate situation worse.

Dad would probably have failed trying to work for someone else. He's an entrepreneur, not an employee. His ultimate success stemmed from the freedom, flexibility, and responsibility that managing his own business allowed him. Successor-managers to a family business need this same freedom because the entrepreneurial spirit is a critical part of their successful de-

velopment. If they're forced too long to work under the owner's watchful (and somewhat prejudiced) eye, it's unlikely they'll work any better than the hired hands they are.

A retirement where the owner-manager retains control over the activities of his supposedly qualified successors is no retirement at all.

4) Real Retirement fits the needs and desires of The Boss's spouse.

Unfortunately, usually the last person considered in the process of "retirement" planning is the spouse of the retiree. In most family businesses, this spouse happens to be a wife, but the problem applies equally to the husband of a retiring woman. The question has to be asked: whose career change is this, anyway?

Too often, I'm approached by wives of business owners who confess their concern about Old Dad's plans. "He's talking about retirement, and I just don't know what I'm going to do with him if he does."

These women have built their own lives while Dad was busy building his business. They have careers, they have volunteer activities, they have their friends and their grandchildren. In some cases, they work in the family business and want to keep doing so. But Dad gets it into his head that it's time to move to Florida, or travel around the world, or go fishing (Mom, of course, stays in the cabin and cooks). Needless to say, none of these ideas holds an automatic attraction for Mom. Not only does she suspect they're not right for Dad, she's also positive they're not right for her.

Dad's probably going to have to find a new career, and that's going to have some effect on Mom. She should have a lot to say about what career Dad might want to choose and what the effect will be on her. Retirees, like successors, come in couples.

THE 10 COMMANDMENTS OF RETIREMENT

These are the problems, challenges, and requirements of that bittersweet stage of life called "retirement." It's at once a curse, a necessity, an unlikely event, and a misnomer. It should probably be called something else — renaissance, renewal, career change — but the term we give to it isn't as important as how we approach it.

Each of us — whether we are business owners, heirs, successors, or spouses, — should keep before us these "10 Commandments of Retirement:"

I. THOU SHALT NEVER RETIRE.

Seems like a contradiction to make the first commandment of retirement an order not to do so, but that's the way it is.

II. THOU SHALT NOT STAY FOREVER IN THY JOB.

this is a sort of converse of Commandment I. The decision not to stop doing doesn't imply continuing what's being done today. Professional firms have an unwritten rule about career potential: "Up or out." For the business owner, it should read "Up and out, and on and on." Don't quit, but don't stand still either.

Dad should, in short, separate his future from the future of the business he's leaving. If he doesn't do this, his future won't be his to control.

III. THOU SHALT TEACH THOSE WHO FOLLOW, BUT NEVER, NEVER CONSIDER IT SUFFICIENT.

In the best of all possible worlds, the older generation passes its wisdom and experience on to the younger generation. This is fine, and a wonderful thing.

It's also next to impossible for parents to do for children.

Any father, for example, who's tried to teach his son how to drive learned very quickly how difficult it is to *teach* ones own offspring. And if it's tough to teach the simple skill of driving, how much less likely will it be that Dad can teach his heirs how to run the business?

If and when we find ourselves frustrated by our students, it is a far, far better thing we do to leave their training to someone else. The best teachers know when to back away from the student.

What's wrong with a little frustration, you might ask? What's wrong is the inevitable suspicion that the student is inept, maybe stupid, and definitely rebellious and disrespectful. There's nothing the matter with kids today that wasn't natural for kids in any day. The "matter" is the tired eyes of the teacher who can't get beyond memories of early mistakes to see his student in an ever-widening light.

IV. THOU SHALT PROVIDE FOR COMPETENT TEACHING OF THY HEIRS.

A direct consequence of Commandment III (the hint that we might be inappropriate teachers for our offspring) is the need to find somebody else to do the job. In the case of the family business these teachers can be other business owners, professional managers within the company, and/or qualified, competent outside directors. This subject will be covered in more detail in Chapter 9.

(It would be nice, of course, if Dad could find students of his own, because he has much to teach and it's good for him to do so. And he'll be amazed at how much better students *other* people's kids can make. By the way, for some reason, grandchildren make *great* students.)

V. THOU SHALT SEEK THE ADVICE, COUNSEL, AND AGREEMENT OF THY SPOUSE.

Just as successors come as couples, so do business owners. None of us operate in a vacuum, nor are we islands of career planning unto ourselves. We do things together, or we're probably not going to do them at all (not for very long, anyway).

This isn't to say that retirement should be a joint career for Dad and Mom. If they don't have a joint career prior to "retirement," there's no particular reason why they should have one after retirement. After all, what they're moving to probably won't be all that different from what they're leaving. Each has a life to lead, only now there may be more time available to do things together.

VI. THOU SHALT AVOID SEEKING WHAT THOU AVOIDED IN THE PAST.

We do what we like and prefer, most of us. If there's a dream that's never really been chased — writing that book, developing that hobby, building that ferro-concrete boat for sailing around the world — there's probably a reason why. Don't expect things to change all of a sudden. It's possible, but the odds are slim.

VII. THOU SHALT AVOID "SEMI-RETIREMENT."

This is a solution many a business owner has hit upon as the answer to his retirement dilemma. It's really little more than an underhanded way to hold onto his job until the Ultimate Boss punches his timecard. It can also have the side effect of fooling the successors and heirs into thinking something positive has happened — until, of course, "He's BACK!"

Semi-retirement is a snare and a delusion.

VIII. THOU SHALT BE COMFORTABLE WITH THE NEED TO PROTECT THY INVESTMENTS.

It's tough sometimes to break habits and values that have been operating for decades, but the risk/reward system does not operate the same for the old as it does for the young and it's important to become more comfortable with a growing preference for the reward end of the equation as one grows older. Risk is for youth. Young people can recover from losses that would be near-terminal for people in their sixties and seventies.

Some owner-managers find it tough to admit or accept that they're no longer risk takers. They start talking instead about "controlled" growth or "dynamic stability," filling the air with all sorts of confusing signals. Conservatism with one's resources is not a sign of decline. It's a common sense result of changing priorities with the passage of time.

The reason for retiring is not altruism or to make room for the coming generation. The reason for retiring is to protect financial security and to lengthen the span of a useful and interesting life.

Suspect altruism as a sole motive — it is usually hiding something.

IX. THOU SHALT DISCUSS THY PLANS WITH THY FAMILY.

They have more than a passing interest.

X. THOU SHALT FOLLOW THY PLAN.

And that's the hard part.

What is usually called "retirement" is not the end of something. It's a continuation of the development process that begins at birth. The difference is an emphasis that changes with time. Early in life, the job we have is to acquire experience in a world that is entirely unknown. Later, we have to learn to break free of the overhanging mass of our experiences and find new worlds to explore. Our taste for complexity and multiplicity of projects declines. Quality becomes more important. Our time horizons narrow, but the view around us improves to magnificence.

Retirement is not something that "happens" to us. It is something we do — and had better do well — because coming back is never really going to be an answer.

Section III

THE PROCESS

Chapter 7
PLANNING THE FUTURE
"Plan? Sure, We Got a Plan . . . Somewhere."

> *Obscurity often brings safety.*
>
> **Aesop**

It's time, now, to move beyond discussion of the "people" in family business and consider a subject with an even more direct impact on succession, management transition, and business survival: planning.

First a fact: If you own a business, you probably don't have a business plan. Lots of *intentions,* maybe. Possibly a few budget objectives, and a new product slowly taking shape under a tarp out in the shop. But not a plan. Not a *real* plan.

So what? Look at our bank balance, you respond. Look at our growth. Look at the way our customers keep coming back. We know exactly where we're going.

Most likely, you do — over the next couple of quarters, maybe even the next year. But what about the year after that? The next *five* years.?

No, you answer again, getting annoyed. We don't know that. But who can?

If you're like most owner-managers, you think of planning as a sort of voodoo, a crystal-ball gazing of the most self-delusionary sort. The world changes too fast. There's too little information. And there's too much to do. Who's got the time, anyway?

Well, let me state a few critical facts right up front:

1) *Success is as much a product of good strategic thinking and positioning as it is of hard work and sheer talent.* This isn't a platitude. It's a research result.

2) *The reality of change is one of the few unchanging realities of business life.* Markets, products, customers, businesses, and whole economies change over time. It's possible even for a "small" business to have advance warning about these changes, because early warning signs do exist.

3) *These early warning signs can be defined and measured by the smaller business, and taking them into account can make significant differences in growth and profits.* This is another research result.

THE "SYMPTOMS" OF FAILURE TO PLAN

For most family companies, the future resides somewhere just a few days past next weekend. "Long range" is usually the end of the next quarter. As common as this is, it's actually contrary to the popular perception. There've been a lot of complaints about America's professional managers and their myopia. But few people think of the business owner as a short-range thinker. It's his money. He has only to answer to himself for his actions, not greedy, impersonal stockholders. He can afford to think longer term.

And so one would think. It does seem that the business owner should be free from a lot of the short-term pressures that plague managers of public corporations. He doesn't have financial analysts to please. He doesn't have stock prices to support through steadily growing profits and dividends. He has the luxury to think in the long term.

Yet he doesn't. Why?

Well, the truth, as any business owner would gladly explain, is that such freedom is an illusion. Closely held companies are severely limited in personnel, funds, and management energy. They generally operate on relatively thin market veneers and are subject to sudden shifts, wild production cycles, intense (but short-lived) brush fires, unexpected reversals, and equally unexpected opportunities. In short, smaller companies find it difficult, if not impossible, to spare anybody from the trenches to give any thought to the long range conduct of the war.

The argument is compelling: What good is long-range thinking if you get your head blown off in the short range process?

Not much, but then what's the alternative? Consider what the *absence* of a business plan usually means:

1) Heirs, as potential successors, have little idea what kind of career future the business represents.

As far as the next generation is concerned, the future will simply look like more of the past and present. We can forgive the heirs if this prospect doesn't fire the imagination.

2) Their spouses, those powerful in-laws, have no concrete manifestation of "The Dream" to reassure them in times of frustration and discouragement.

If the business seems to be going nowhere, who can blame them for not wanting to go along with it?

3) Management — including The Boss, the successors, the non-family key executives, and even the hapless hourly "help" — continually and increasingly are at the mercy of the environment.

Who can blame the blind and exhausted for stumbling off the edge of a precipice?

4) There are no standards for qualifying successor management for the future other than the standards of the past.

Without a plan for the business future, potential successors will be immersed in management *history* through most of their formative period. Why should anybody be surprised if these new managers turn out to be incapable of handling change and growth.

5) There can be no schedule or deadline for management transition.

Without a plan, transition becomes a someday thing — "someday, when they're ready, but not yet. Not yet." Small wonder why the best word to describe a successor is "frustrated."

6) Retirement of the present owner(s) is all but impossible.

Who could turn their back on all these brushfires, especially when there's nowhere to go — and nobody else around who's prepared to fight them?

7) Outside advice and help have little impact on the company and its managers.

Advisers and directors tend to ask questions like "Where can we help you go?" and "What is it you want to do?" Without a plan, those questions can't really be answered.

Success, unfortunately, tends to hide all of these symptoms — at least until it's almost too late to reverse them.

Success isn't the only problem. Most business owners see very early that a major benefit of business ownership is flexibility. Their smaller size allows quick maneuvers, fast stops and reversals, and blinding swiftness in pouncing on opportunities. In fact, this flexibility had much to do with their success.

So much for the benefit.

There's also a dangerous side effect of flexibility which not too many business owners recognize: it's addicting. It gives the illusion of freedom and power while it steadily tightens its hold on the business owner's prudence and intelligence. Although flexibility begins as pure advantage, over time it becomes a minor god to the business owner. Over time, anything — or anyone — that even hints at limiting freedom is condemned as representative of Satan.

The business owner regularly and willingly sacrifices planning to the god of flexibility. That's *really* why so few closely held businesses have a *real* long-range business plan. Oh, there are a lot of showpieces out there — you know, put together for bankers or drawn up at seminars, but almost invariably these wind up as thick, dusty tomes leaning unused on a conspicuous shelf somewhere.

Countless business "plans" have been drawn up through the expensive labor of consultants (or, more likely these days, through the frustrated labor of would-be successors), only to be ignored, or worse, disdained by the entrenched management.

"Fine," The Boss and his henchmen say when The Plan is presented. "That's an impressive piece of work. Now let's get back to making money."

WHY MOST "PLANS" JUST GATHER DUST

The problem with planning in the smaller company is actually two problems. The "establishment" has little taste for it ("we did pretty well without it up till now"), while the successor managers have too much. (Successors often view planning as a panacea, and this "misplaced" enthusiasm is clearly obvious to the older managers. With a mild sigh, they tolerate it as a manifestation of managerial puberty.)

The result? Well, the managers who have the energy and inclination to plan, lack the power to implement. Those who lack the inclination to plan, have the power to implement.

Sometimes, a plan does get finished under these conditions, but it's an effort generally doomed from the outset to be stillborn. The copies get made and distributed. The successor is satisfied (at first) and expectant.

Ultimately, of course, the plan is totally ignored.

Successors keep volunteering, though, even if they suspect nothing will come of their efforts. What else is there to do? As far as the establishment seems to think, the heirs are useless in the trenches. They haven't been trained in tactics. They don't know how to keep their heads down. If they want to plan, let them plan, the "sergeant" figures. It"ll keep them out of the way.

So they remain behind the lines to do whatever it is they do when they plan. Later, plan in hand, they crawl up to the front and expect Dad and the old guard to turn their backs on the whizzing bullets to read and react to the *Magnum Opus*.

Even Jimmy the Greek wouldn't bother to give odds on that one.

There *are* a lot of convincing reasons for failing to plan. Reality *does* make it difficult. The pace of change in today's world makes long-range thinking seem as fruitless as trying to build a sandcastle at the bottom of a river. For all of these reasons — and more — few family companies plan.

Yet, somehow, we're going to have to find some planning handholds in the sheer cliff of business ownership and haul ourselves into the future.

Whatever the dangers and inconveniences, remember the long and deadly drop in the other direction.

Preliminary almost to everything in developing a family business plan is a massive promotional campaign. Whoever chooses (or is chosen) to bear the planning cross will first have to find a way to persuade the other managers (and the shareholders) that tomorrow is, in fact, worth thinking about. The business is accelerating and gaining altitude. The people flying it are going to have to get off the shiny seats of their pants and begin building an instrument panel.

The weather isn't going to get clearer.

Maybe this persuasion will be easier in the '80s. Almost every competent manager realizes he must understand the "visual rules" of tactics — skirting storms, avoiding collisions, and so forth — but today more than ever he also needs to know how to operate in areas where he can't see directly. Maybe the "interesting" events of recent years have iced the windshields often enough and quickly enough to teach a lesson. But whether the scare has taken or not, every manager must learn how to follow the instrument rules of strategy or he, his business, and any "passengers" luckless enough to depend on him are in mortal danger.

It's probably going to be a tough sell, though. Old school barnstormers like the founding entrepreneur and his old guard escadrille have an inbred distrust of "instruments." They've survived with nerves of steel, daring, superb reflexes, and a lot of luck. Strategy, to them, feels a lot like a crutch for people who don't know how to run a business.

Such opinions are understandable — and dead wrong. "Dead wrong" isn't the statement of a glib prejudice, but the conclusion reached by students of business and management throughout the world. If we want more concrete, less ivory tower evidence, we need only to travel to Tokyo.

Fortunately, (and contrary to the convictions of our entrepreneurial "aces") strategic management is as possible in the closely held business as it is necessary. I'll restate, for emphasis, the facts of business life listed earlier in the chapter:

1) *Success is as much a product of good strategic thinking and positioning as it is of hard work and sheer talent. This isn't a platitude. It's a research result.*

2) *The reality of change is one of the few unchanging realities of business life. Markets, products, customers, businesses, and whole economies change over time. It's possible even for a "small" business to have advance warning about these changes, because early warning signs do exist.*

3) *These early warning signs can be defined and measured by the smaller business, and taking them into account can make significant differences in growth and profits.*

The above seems to imply that hard work isn't enough for success. But hard work and sheer talent are what made the founder what he is. Aren't they? It's the sweat equity that built the business, isn't it? How can we now say they're not important?

The careful reader will, of course, realize that nothing's been said to imply that hard work or ability aren't important. They're just not *sufficient* for a successful, growing business. Businesses change and so do their management needs.

Hardly anybody would deny that business founders who've succeeded had to work longer, quicker, harder, and more relentlessly than their competitors — and most everybody else. But that's not the whole story, even if The Boss would like to think so. In addition to working harder and faster, he was also thinking smarter and deeper than his competition. We all know a lot of people who work hard. Why is it that only a few of them actually succeed the way the successful business founder has?

The trouble The Boss and his henchmen fall into over time is that they lose their gut understanding of their marketplace. The markets change. The old customers change. The owners get farther and farther away from the street where they learned their strategy in the first place. They begin to lose touch and, therefore, the good positioning they had. To make up for this, they begin to work harder and harder. They forget about good thinking and begin to deify hard work.

But no matter how much entrepreneurs ignore it or how vehemently they deny the fact, perceptive market segmentation, careful investment strategy, charted reinvestment policies, and smart positioning are important to both the founding entrepreneur *and* to the successful owner-manager. They're even *more* important, in fact, as markets mature and businesses succeed. These things might all sound like academic jargon to the owner-manager, but the fact is, he did all of them in the beginning, and he did them smart.

Despite what The Boss says, his success wasn't due to doing the right things the right way. In the beginning he had the sense, even the genius, to do the right things. That's true. The fact that he probably did them all wrong didn't matter so much because he was the only one who was at least on the right track — and his hard work bailed out his mistakes. Later, with success (which increases the complexity of his life, his business, and his competition), he begins to lose even that advantage, losing sight of the right things to do in the confusion of change. He continues, instead, with all he has left: concentration on "doing" rather than "rightness."

He sees this as the lesson of experience. His younger managers, particularly his heirs, see it as downright stubbornness. What it really is for the entrepreneur is a subtle shift into neutral.

SYMPTOMS OF THE "IDLING" COMPANY

If any owner-manager wants to know if he's fallen into this trap, he can run a little self-diagnosis. A "yes" answer to any of the following questions should run a large flapping red flag up the business flagpole:

1) Does my accounting system serve more to "elasticize" results than to clarify the truth?

While the tax system in this country demands that every business have at least a rudimentary accounting system, the tax structure also leads business owners into ever more creative approaches to breaking even at a higher level every year. If your accounting system is designed more to frustrate the obnoxious agent than to provide unadorned, honest management information, you're not running a business. You're running a tax shelter.

2) Is my business heavily supporting non-productive activities, or departments, or employees?

If it is, you'll know exactly what I mean by "non-productive." How "business" are the business expenses? Just how much "salary" is in management salaries? Entrepreneurs build. Idling entrepreneurs harvest.

3) Is the average age of the key managers closer to retirement age than youth?

Entrepreneurs surround themselves with workhorses, arm themselves with bullwhips, and mush ahead at all deliberate speed — until, that is, they've been driving the team for a couple of decades or more. As the driver ages, so does the team. Unless new blood has been added, the decline in energy, interest, and speed will hardly be noticeable to the incumbents. They're still working like hell, by their standards, at any rate.

4) Am I indulging in expensive hobbies?

By this, I don't mean stamp collecting or wild animal photography. The expensive hobbies of the "idling" entrepreneur tend to be new business "ventures." Unrelated acquisitions in faddish new growth areas are an almost sure sign that the entrepreneur has become bored with his core business and is using it as a cash cow to rekindle the embers of his economic youth.

5) Am I starting to long for "controlled" growth?

Strategic management requires the taking of risk. The growing taste for holding fast and controlling growth is a symptom of managerial retirement because real risk is the very essence of entrepreneurship.

The successors, by the way, aren't immune to this kind of managerial catatonia. One of the dangers of living in The Boss's shadow is growing up with his peculiar twists, slants, and branches. If he's the only teacher, his student can almost imperceptibly fall victim to "entrepreneurial cloning," an overlearning at The Boss's sizable knee. If this has happened, the successor(s) can be idling along with The Boss. How to know? Ask the same five questions.

Family business managers must unretire, and stay that way. The world is changing and the company must change with it to survive.

THE SIGNS OF CHANGE — AND WHAT THEY MEAN

Every closely held business operates in an ecological niche. It hammers out its particular place to fit into the surrounding economy and then specializes to survive and grow in that niche. So far, so good . . . until the environment changes.

Success or failure are functions of more than internal factors. Changes within the business itself are important, of course, but they don't happen independently of the environment, which effects every business in powerful and far-reaching ways. All sorts of external changes are occurring all the time. Customers enter and leave the market. Suppliers adjust product lines, prices and distribution policies. Competition heats up, cools off, becomes more and less aggressive. No business can long remain aloof from these changes.

Sailing hard through this environmental squall, each business also goes through an internal storm of its own, partially in response to the changing environment and partially in response to progression through its own life cycle. Business planning, and the succession planning it precedes, require the anticipation of these changes and adaptation to them.

Markets change in fairly typical ways with time. The orientation of mangers within those markets must change, too, as should management style. Much of this change is predictable, and simply by observing the nature of the market or the style of the managers, the changing position and corresponding needs of the business can be determined.

These changes can be superb measures of business and managerial evolution, sort of like fixed landmarks along the planning landscape. But they can also be telltale signs of failure to adapt to change. Standards of evolution and change are set by the average, the typical company and typical manager. The family company, however, tends to freeze the typical evolution and try to avoid the cycle altogether.

But change can't be avoided. Although it sometimes can be postponed a little, the price is high — almost total lack of preparation for the inevitable change when it finally does come.

It's worth taking a few lines to consider how markets and managers typically change:

Changes in Markets. New markets tend to be building at the expense of old markets, usually because the new market involves fewer direct competitors, each of whom are energetically seeking recognition for their unique products or services. An aging market, in fact, can be defined as one that's losing business to newer markets. Competition in an aging market is no longer well defined and tends to come as much from outside the market as within. Growth and success come to those who are able to cash in on aging markets in order to enter new ones.

Market aging hits a business with a double punch — new competition and new strategic requirements. Most of the strategies which once made the company successful in its new market later become inappropriate. Whether or not the managers recognize the difference, the market is not going to stop changing. If they "idle" in the glow of success, their company will simply be left behind.

Changes in Management Orientation. To be successful, a business must consistently renew itself. New markets arise from new products and services, which come from companies with driving innovative energy and product-oriented managers. These innovators fix, improve, change — anything to make the product more exciting or palatable to the customer.

That's all fine for businesses in new markets, but as their market reorients and ages, these companies begin to require their managers to change. To continue to be appropriate to their markets, they have to progress from product orientation through, first, a preoccupation with marketing and production and then, later, to a concern for finance — staying profitable in a declining business.

That's the ideal. It's not unusual in real life to find owner-managers who refuse to leave their product orientation (which is always more fun) for the less exciting and more demanding (to them) market, production, and financial concerns. As I discussed in Chapter 5, there's a lot of evidence which implies that entrepreneurs shouldn't try to manage successful businesses. In most cases, their skills are much better used in doing what they like to do: building new businesses.

They can't do either, however, with their drive train in neutral.

Management Style. Here's where the entrepreneur most drastically parts company with the changing needs of his business and the marketplace. Typically, founders are personally involved in operations. They're creative and emotionally involved with the product. Growth and success, however, bring with them needs for managers skilled in fine tuning and long-range thinking. The organization becomes too large and complex for the shirtsleeves management so appropriate in the beginning.

Most of this is effectively ignored by the idling owner-manager. He, along with his managers and students (the ones who survive, at least) — tend, instead, to settle comfortably into the product-oriented, personal management style of the risk-taker. The problem is *the business is successful*. The risk has been taken and it worked out. Now the aging company needs managers, not risk-takers, but where are they?

The reason planning has so much to do with continued success is the fact that it *forces* the managers to define which markets are aging and which are new. It *forces* managers to think about their business as *many* businesses, some new, some growing, and some aging. It *forces* managers to plan for the needs of each of these segments — and find the appropriate people to run them.

In most cases, The Boss isn't idling because he desperately wants to retire. He's idling because he's a risk-taker stuck in a growing business and forced to manage a style he dislikes and for which he has little talent. Looked at in this way, the family company can potentially accommodate a lot of differences in management style. In fact, it *needs* those differences.

This has some really important implications concerning "retirement," which I've already discussed. But it also begins to clarify why business planning is central to succession planning.

WHY A PLAN IS ESSENTIAL TO SUCCESSION

Without a long-range, workable business plan, management succession in a closely held business is an almost hopeless, frequently painful dream. Whether we like it or not, the business plan functions as the keystone of every successful succession plan. If the plan doesn't exist, or if it's poorly done, the other components of the transition process will trip and stumble helplessly over each other.

Management succession happens "tomorrow," to be sure, but it's a flower deeply rooted in what happens today. Everybody plans for the flower, watching and waiting for it to bloom. They build their lives and their financial futures around it — and all the while, they ignore the needs it has in the present. The edifice of the dream is built with an eye on how it's going to look. Later, when the family tries to live in that building, they realize someone forgot to install the plumbing.

Without a management strategy and a long-range plan, successful management transition is unlikely to occur. Oh, something will happen. Businesses don't simply vanish. But much of the true potential, both human and economic, represented by the successful closely held business will be wasted if transition is attempted without planning.

To some this might seem a bold and bald statement. And, surely, there will always be exceptions — some companies might just be able to pull themselves out of the tailspin in time to survive. Buy most of us possess neither the necessary genius nor the fantastic level of luck required. For most of us, planning is *essential* to management and ownership transition.

Management succession is required, obviously, because managers are mortal. But mortality shouldn't be the reason succession planning is done. It only defines why succession is inevitable. Transition can, and often does, happen without planning.

Succession planning is critical, instead, because the business cycle affects the appropriateness of the various management styles. If these changes aren't understood, defined, and provided for, the business will almost inevitably limp steadily into a swamp of managerial confusion and frustration. The wrong people with the wrong skills will be in the wrong jobs at the wrong times. That's a lot of "wrongs."

Succession is very much a life-cycle phenomenon, and the need for it usually comes about at one of the most difficult points on that life cycle — the maturity stage or peak of business development. This is the time that some of the most profound changes are beginning to occur, changes which tend to have a great personal impact on the people involved.

Just at the time the old business and the old markets are beginning to decline, a family business is being asked to work out its succession problems. In response, the family almost automatically accepts "more of the same" as the answer — more sales, more work, more of Dad's kind of skills. If the successors can't do this, or don't believe in it, or (very likely) it doesn't work, the assumption that the successors are inadequate to the job.

But the real job hasn't been defined. Without a business plan, there's no real basis for deciding what skills are needed and where.

A lot of adaptation is required when a business matures, and to do this the people involved have to anticipate and understand what changes are occurring. Aging products and markets, for example, often require changes in product line, noteably lowering of price and maybe quality. A move to private branding might be required, with the consequent loss of product identification.

If a company is operating strategically and following a business plan, these sorts of changes are expected and anticipated. Without a plan, they come as unpleasant surprises —and are met with resistance from the surprised managers.

But aging products and markets also imply the need for new products in new markets. A business plan will also disclose these needs and anticipate them. Is The Boss upset about watching products in decline? Then why not put him to work on what he does best anyway — building new products, opening new markets? With him where he belongs, we can search the heirs and key managers for people with the talents and skills to manage the mature business, thus assuring a continued flow of cash to the new ventures.

Without a plan, managers react to change rather than anticipate it. And when they react, they react fairly typically along generational lines. Conservatism struggles with aggressiveness. Stability fights risk-taking. *Nowhere in the growing conflict is there a recognition that these are complements, not opposites.*

The old guard, by this time, have been at the helm for an entire generation — 25 years and more. Egos are strongly involved in the company and the decisions made for it over the years. Adapting to change requires questioning of those decisions.

It's the future, not the past that's being questioned, but without a plan, that's not obvious. Instead, people think they're being questioned personally, and they resist. They maintain, rightly to some extent, that the experience and wisdom they've gained over the years are priceless assets. What they forget is the learning process that went on gaining that experience and wisdom. The first generation didn't build on the past any more or less than successors will — or should.

The successors, for their part, enter the business "naked on the half-shell," so to speak. For all the reasons explained in Chapter 1, they have no significant ballast of experience. Nor do they have any significant loyalty to the decisions of the past — quite naturally, they weren't even around. As is the general nature of youth, they want change and they see it as their only potential road to credibility and success. Doing more of what the present management is doing, they reason, will only serve to keep them under the old guard's thumb. So instead of working toward conflict resolution, the successors (consciously or not) are agitating for management revolution. They have, without a plan, no more concept of their place in the life cycle than the previous generation does.

Oh, they talk about planning, all right, but for them it's more of a weapon than a joint solution to a common problem.

Small wonder the old guard in the trenches pay little attention.

Business planning is a communal process and it involves every thread in the fabric of the business. Without it, the process of succession meanders ineffectually on a flat, trackless terrain.

THE ESSENTIAL COMPONENTS OF A FAMILY BUSINESS PLAN

While it is far beyond the scope of this book to describe the detailed process of preparing a business plan, there are some fundamental steps in the process that are useful to discuss. This book is about succession planning, and business planning is a keystone of that process. Clearly, some understanding of the shape of that keystone is essential to making succession work.

First, a word needs to be said about involving, everybody in the plan. A business plan will not work if it doesn't have the agreement, support, and consensus of all the key people in the company, and it won't have that support if they weren't involved to some extent in the plan's development. The successor might initiate the process — a typical, and quite natural role —

but it's crucial that he or she bring others into the process as soon as practically possible.

There are four basic phases or stages in planning. Each builds on the last and they must necessarily come in order.

Stage 1 — *The Business Analysis and Profile*.

The first step in any planning process is to "review the situation." This means an examination of the market, the trends and changes that have occurred and are going on. What's happening to competition, to market share, and the company's own market position? Are sales increasing or decreasing — and how do we really know? Have we accounted for inflation? Do we understand our investment strategy? How is the company performing? Where is it in its life cycle? Which markets are growing and which are declining?

The real question in this initial stage is whether or not we understand our present business strategy. It might seem obvious, particularly to the business owner and the old guard, but a good test of whether or not it's actually understood is to ask all the key people, particularly the successor managers, to give their definitions of the strategy. Nine times out of ten, this attempt at explanation will fail. It will deteriorate into a series of mumbled "youknowwhatImean's."

Before any viable planning can be done, every key manager in the company must have a clear idea about three things: (1) the company's served market, (2) the company's competitive advantage, and (3) the company's greatest strength. And those "clear ideas" must agree, key manager to key manager, owner-manager to successor-manager. They probably won't agree initially, and some will have to change in coming to an agreement, but all of the managers have to share the same fundamental concept of the company. That's the only real foundation for a working plan.

Stage 2 — *Evaluation of Alternatives*.

Once present strategy is defined, it's time to do a little zero-based investment analysis. A primary question for the future is whether or not we should reinvest in the present business.

Too many companies take the answer to this question for granted, and assume it is "yes."

First of all, in a family company, this issue is not quite as straightforward as it is in larger public companies because the *family* is part of the reason the business is in business. In other words, family companies are often used as generators of "pseudo-dividends," shareholder perquisites, and family income security. Reinvestment will almost always cut into these objectives.

But, also, there are important questions of business strength and market attractiveness. A mature business in a mature market is not necessarily the best place to invest funds. In fact, it might better be used as a generator of funds for other, more attractive (in the long term) businesses.

The "pseudo-dividend" issues are important as a background, sort of setting the "key" for business planning. They have to be laid out on the shareholders' table, discussed intelligently and rationally, and then folded into the long-range investment decisions. This, as most family businesses soon realize, is a tough discussion to start, keep going, and survive. I won't go into it here because it's discussed in detail in the next chapter. But it should be remembered that it needs to be done, and it must be accomplished.

The business reinvestment decision is a little more straightforward and less emotional (but not necessarily easier). The business reinvestment decision revolves around questions of industry and market attractiveness, competitive advantage, and business strengths.

* Is our industry a good one to be in (e.g. compare the long-term prospects of the steel industry to those of telecommunications)? Is the marketplace open to future growth or is it saturated and highly competitive?

* Is our lead in this industry wide enough and secure enough to assure long-term growth, or will competition soon begin taking away our customers?

* Are we using all our strengths? Is our unique skill really

our greatest strength — and will it last? Are there other strengths we can develop?

The investment decision, of course, will revolve around the security concerns of the present management, as well as their confidence and trust in the next generation. All of this has to be analyzed, discussed, and taken into consideration when the closely held company begins to make investment and strategy decisions for the future.

Stage 3 — *Deciding on a Strategic Position.*

This is probably the most creatively demanding of the planning stages, because it involves "reincarnation" of the stroke of genius that began the company's success. "We did it once, now we gotta do it again. What kind of business are we going to build?"

A number of alternatives and combinations of alternatives are available:

* The company could concentrate on adapting to change in the industry and market, finding growing segments and leaving declining segments.

* The company could capitalize on its particular strengths and advantages, improve new ones, and overcome weaknesses.

* Finally, the company can decide to turn its attention elsewhere, using the present business as a cash cow to fund new and more productive businesses.

Stage 4 — *Putting the Plan to Work.*

In a sense, this is the easiest part of business planning, because it gets back to what the managers understand: action. It will also have a very beneficial effect on personal relationships among the shareholders and the managers. At least there will be an agreed direction for the future *and defined roles for the successor-managers.*

Here are the key steps in implementing the plan:

* Write out a statement of the basic philosophy behind the plan. What direction is the company going? What's the extent of the goal? On what strengths will the future be built, and how will those strengths assure success?

* Set some realistic, measurable, and concrete criteria for meeting the goals of the plan. The better defined these are, the easier it will be to reach objectives — and realize it when you get there.

* Write out a detailed *tactical* plan for reaching those concrete criteria for success, including the responsibilities of the various groups and defining who is going to do what and when.

* Put together financial projections to cover the duration of the plan, with a special emphasis on sources and uses of funds.

THE 5 POSITIVE EFFECTS OF PLANNING

It should be obvious by now that business planning isn't a one-time project. Putting the first coherent plan together will probably involve some significant concentration of effort — after all, there's probably a lot of neglect to make up for — and once the plan is in place, the review of it should be ongoing.

A defined management strategy, kept flexible and adapted to inevitable change, is going to provide the backbone of the overall succession plan. If the strategy is weak, or inflexible, or not accepted by everybody, it's flaws will be reflected in larger flaws in the plan for management transition and continuity.

A sound management strategy will:

1) Define the business future and the potential career paths for heirs and outside managers.

In short, people will, for once, have some idea in what direction they're heading.

2) Give the spouses of heirs and successors some written, concrete commitment that something will come of their investment of time and emotion.

This can be a great comfort on cold, lonely nights.

3) Provide real jobs — and real performance measures — for successor-managers.

Accept no substitutes.

4) Help define the process of management and ownership transition and, more importantly, provide a

schedule for its occurrence.

With a sound plan, the present owner(s) can begin to have trust in the idea that succession is, in fact, possible. That can help one get through those cold, lonely nights, too.

5) Make it possible for professional advisers and outside directors to help the company survive and grow.

They will finally have something to work with other than vague dreams, subliminal frustrations, and inadequate data.

Companies have survived management transition without management strategy and a plan. But most who've tried it, didn't. Planning is difficult and becomes important at all the wrong times, but it's as much an investment as the investment of funds in a new venture.

If a business owning family is serious about its commitment to the future, they will make that investment gladly.

Chapter 8
GIVING IT AWAY
"You Don't Even WANT To Take It with You"

No one goes to Hades with all his
immense wealth.
Theognis

It was somewhere in Florida, if my memory is right, at a break in a seminar I was giving on succession planning, that a business owner came up to me with a remarkable story.

"It's a coincidence," he said, "that you were here talking about estate planning. I just changed my plan about a week before coming down here. Signed the papers on my way to the airport."

"Why a change?" I asked.

"To disinherit my older son," he answered.

He let that sink in, for effect, I guess, before responding to my raised eyebrow.

"Well, I didn't really 'disinherit' him. I just made sur that all of my stock will go to my younger son, rather than ha to each as it was before."

"Your older son's not in the company?"

"Oh, yeah," he answered. "He's the president."

Then, again responding to my raised eyebrow:

"Look, my older son and I never agree on anything — and that includes how to run the business. It's gotten to the point where I've had it up to here fighting with him. I don't want him to have any control over the company after I'm gone."

"That's your privilege," I noted, neutrally. "What did your son have to say about it?"

"Oh, I didn't tell him. Why should I? Then all we'd do is fight about *that*."

This approach to assuring the peace, as close as I can tell, boils down to delaying the war until the next generation. It might seem obvious to you that this is dangerous and unwise, yet it's one of the most common sins of omission committed in family companies.

HOW ESTATES GET "OUT OF HAND"

We could spend volumes clucking over almost infinite variations on the estate planning horror story, but we don't have volumes at our disposal. Nevertheless, some "f'ristances" might be useful, if only to demonstrate the horrendous ramifications of simply doing nothing.

Founders build businesses. Successors develop them and keep them alive. That's something we all know. Something many of us *don't* realize, however, is that the successful entrepreneur and his family often have parallel skills at *demolition*. All the while they're building a successful company, they're laying booby traps and detonators in with the brick and mortar. They might take a long time to go off — but go off they do.

An example of a company on the West Coast comes to mind. This is a welding supply business that's now in its fourth generation of family management. A success story on the surface, this company is now showing the spreading cracks from detonations among the family's subterranean bombs. And there seem to be more to come.

The company was founded as a blacksmith shop at the turn of the century and now has a sales volume in excess of $10 million. The president of the company (we'll call him "Bill")

works in the business with his brother. Neither of them has any ownership — what their branch of the family owns (25% of the common stock) is in the hands of their mother. The rest of the stock sits in 12.5% blocks in the hands of the founder's six other great grandchildren.

We'll get to the "cracks" in a moment, but first you should have an understanding of how this interesting ownership distribution came about. Great-granddad had two sons, both of whom worked for him and who, quite naturally, divided the ownership of the business after the old blacksmith's demise.

To this point, it's a typical family business story. Nothing all that unusual, until, about 10 years after the founder died, the two second-generation heirs (Bill's grandfather and granduncle) got into a conflict of some sort (nobody today remembers what it was about), which resulted in Bill's granduncle walking out of the business — taking his 50% along. As a consequence, the ownership of this company is now divided equally among involved and non-involved families. Within living memory, it's never been any other way.

The departure of that 50% block of ownership with Bill's granduncle thickened the plot considerably. That wayward 50% went to an only son, who not long ago divided his shares among four daughters. Bill's grandfather left the half that stayed with the company to Bill's father and Bill's uncle, both of whom worked in the company all their lives. Bill's father then left his shares to his wife, Bill's mother. The uncle's 25% went to two sons who work in the company with Bill.

You may be having a hard time following all this, but you can bet the owners aren't. They think about it all the time.

All the time.

Bill and his brother thought it was okay for their mother to have the stock — until Mom and her daughters-in-law stopped getting along with each other. Miffed and resentful, Mom's presently alternating between threats to put it all in trust for charity and hints of a long-term "liaison" with a retired attorney in Ft. Myers. Bill's uncle — his only ally with any influence over the shareholders — is on the board, but disabled by a major stroke.

The disabled uncle's four shareholder-daughters and Bill's Mom are lobbying for larger dividends. Bill thinks the company should expand. The two ideas are not complementary, and they're definitely not compatible.

Even though Bill has done a great job as the fourth-generation president, his attention and his energy are increasingly concentrated elsewhere. His main worry is not how to be successful, but rather whether he's foolish to build a successful company under the thumb of his shareholder relatives. A few well-formed alliances among the disgruntled, after all, could easily push him out the door.

So much for a well-planned estate.

Another example of the sorry condition of American family business estate planning is a young man I met at a convention in the Northwest. His father had founded their family tile business, had given 5% ownership to each of two key employees, and planned on passing the business on to his son. It didn't happen that way, unfortunately. Dad died "prematurely," before he could get around to changing the share repurchase agreement, and the 10% in non-family hands suddenly became 100%. This is called disinheritance by accident.

So much for a timely estate plan.

WHY ESTATE PLANS ARE NOT — OR BADLY — DONE

Why do otherwise intelligent human beings so often allow their major asset to bounce around helplessly on the wheel of chance? From what I've seen, it's only for the best of reasons. Precisely because they want to do the right thing, they fail, absolutely, to do anything right at all.

Almost without fail, whenever I ask an audience of business owners for a show of hands by those who have a viable, up-to-date estate plan, only five to 10 percent will raise their hands. When I ask, further, how many of *them* have discussed that plan with their heirs, most of those sparsely scattered hands drop quickly.

This almost universal failure is easily understood. In the first place, it's tough talking about estate planning. If Dad brings it up to Mom and the kids, he figures they'll think he's a candidate for open heart surgery. If Mom asks him, he'll probably start wondering if she's really going to bridge club those afternoons she's "out." And the kids — the only reason they'd ask is because they were broke or itching to get their hands on his money.

So who brings it up? Nobody — except Dad's insurance agent or maybe the lawyer.

There's more than simple discomfort involved, though. There's also a lot of doubt in Dad's mind about what's the best thing to do. When he looks at his heirs, he often sees their anxiety and disagreements. He sees their tugging at the traces, longing for "freedom," and wonders if he shouldn't just liquidate and let them loose. But his whole history and background — and his hope — cry against such a solution.

"Someday," as one Mexican business owner said to me, "they will come to their senses and see what it means to have a place to work."

Dad hopes that time and more success will solve the aching confusions within his family. Faced with these two extremes — sale or delay — he almost inevitably chooses to wait.

There'll be some pressure from his advisers if they're worth their fees, but he's not easy to move. "Gee, Joe," Dad will vaguely remember their saying to him a few years back, "you really ought to do something about your estate." He agrees. Of course. It's just that he never gets around to it.

And he's not unique. I wouldn't be surprised if there were hundreds of thousands of carefully constructed estate plans lying around business owners' desks, dusty and *unsigned*.

They'll get around to *those* someday, too.

Sure they will — posthumously. If mediums and "psychics" could only figure out how to make it work, most of the money spent on financial planning would be theirs for transmitting delayed instructions from the Dear Departed. But until the sensitives make this breakthrough, the business owner's desires will too often pass on with him, leaving his advisers to hammer out hasty damage control measures over cold coffee and assorted Danish at The Boss's funeral breakfast.

Why doesn't the business owner plan his or her estate? It's not really to be contrary or to cause problems for the next generation. Those might be the effects of inaction, but usually they're not the owner-manager's real intent. Usually a number of other problems lead him to say "later" to writing his plan for giving away the business:

1) The Desire To Be "Fair."

Business owners, like most human parents, love their children equally and have equivalent concerns for the welfare of each. So, when it comes to thinking about an estate plan that's "fair," they tend to think in terms of "equal." Why else would there be so many second-generation family companies owned in equal parts by involved and non-involved siblings?

Is "equal" "fair"? Here's how it works: Joe owns half, does all the work, and takes out all the money. Sister Kate owns half, lives a thousand miles away and does none of the work, and takes out none of the money. Guess who becomes a thorn in whose side — and who feels who is unfairly sharing in whose hard-won equity growth.

Sometimes "fair" is defined as leaving the business to Mother. Let her decide — at least we've made sure the kids will be nice to her in her fading years. The way this "works" is: rotating presidencies, hobbled successor-managers, insecure widows who control businesses rather than money, and (not *that* infrequently) suave gigolos hot on the trail of a "good thing."

"Fair" can be achieved in lots of creative, if irrational, ways — usually involving some variation on the equality theme. However, the concern for evenhandedness, amplified by emotion and love, too often overwhelms the whispered advice of logic and business sense.

But don't think this fair/equal dilemma is lost on The Boss. After all, he didn't get where he is by being stupid or insensitive to nuance. No, he often sees all too clearly that there's a major conflict between what's fair for his family and what's good for the business. He can opt for one or the other option out of sheer exhaustion, or he can decide to wait. Maybe something will come up to clarify matters.

Maybe. I understand Germany was waiting for a secret weapon, too.

2) Doubts about the Successors.

(Or, as a corollary, their doubts about The Boss.) How can the business owner decide how — not to mention when — to pass on management and control of his business when the real leader (read "Dad's Clone") hasn't emerged, or the young-sters aren't ready, or they don't get along, or he doesn't trust that brute his daughter married? How can he decide to give up control of his company when Junior keeps buying antique Jag-uars, or wanting to invest in the Mexican Peso, or making mid-night trips to Vegas?

"I know we've always been in the beer business, Dad, but computer software is where it's at today. That's the business we should be in."

How'd Dad supposed to decide under those conditions?

He's not. And he won't. Period.

I've seen business owners stand firm on their inaction, year after year, bending nary a little under the gale of dire warn-ings from advisers and succesors about "liquidity problems," the predictable disasters that are going to happen when Uncle Sam's goon squads descend on the disorganized, freshly opened estate.

"The business is going to go under, Dad!"

"Says who?" he asks, his mind working, thinking: *Be-sides, maybe there wouldn't be such a problem if you took that $250,000 salary of yours and left it in the company.*

Dad knows there's a problem when there is one, but sometimes in his righteous anger he decides it isn't *his* problem. Instead, maybe it's somebody else's just deserts — the Lord's way of righting a wrong, so to speak.

I've seen owner-managers, year after year, pushing aside sound tax advice because they "want to see what (or whether) Junior decides to do" or "need more time to observe the two of them as managers" or "want to be sure that bum isn't going to walk out on my daughter."

Most other professional advisers have seen it, too, much to their frustration. Old Dad just won't move.

But, then, would *you*, under the same circumstances?

3) An Overdeveloped Sense of Personal Longevity.

When it happens, each of us will be convinced we died prematurely. It's only others who so generously reflect that "He had a full life."

For many reasons, the business owner is more prone to this sort of assumed immortality than most lesser humans. He's *always been busy.* He's *always* been successful. He's *always* worked hard. It's almost impossible for him to imagine anything different.

Often, the business owner's procrastination is due in part (if not in total) to his unwavering conviction that there's time to get it done, plenty of time. Estate planning just doesn't seem all that urgent, especially not with all the business problems he has to solve *today.* Hell, if we don't survive this recession, what good's an estate plan going to do?

He'll do it "later," and there's always going to be a later.

4) "My business is different."

Nobody really understands The Boss's problems, see? There may be answers for other companies, The Boss often thinks, and, sure, there are a lot of smart lawyers and people like that out there — but none of that really applies to me. His situation is so complex that 10 years of worry and thought on his part haven't even begun to unravel a solution. How is some smart, but uninformed, adviser or consultant going to do it?

If his business were, in fact, that different, then his conclusions would be justified. But this book, by itself, should be enough evidence of how *undifferent* most family businesses are from each other — a fortunate fact, actually, at least for estate planning purposes. Imagine, for example, what the world of medicine would be like if every human body were different — different organs, tissues, blood. With every sickness, the entire body of medical knowledge would have to be rediscovered. Health care would be hokus pokus, mostly self-delivered. It would be a world in which you would sue *yourself* for malpractice.

Family businesses *are* different from each other in many ways, but the differences aren't quantum leaps. They are variations on some fairly well-understood themes, and there's precedent for most every situation. Over the centuries, a body of law and practice has accumulated that is flexible enough to handle most every situation, no matter how complex or unique the problems might seem to the protagonists.

Unfortunately, too few business owners accept the possibility that somebody else might have the answers to questions they've been asking themselves for years. Instead, they draw the blinds even tighter and withdraw into their own worries. They consult the only oracle they know — themselves — and the answer, almost invariably, is "we're workin' on it."

Business owners aren't the only people alone with their internal prophets. Their heirs go through a lot of temple haunting of their own, although with one very important difference. The heirs actually go out and *look* for ideas. Most of the time, however, they limit their search to books and specialized seminars. They want to do it themselves, partially because they have no greater love for paying professional fees than Dad does, but partially, too, because they have a suspicion that the solution they would like to see is not the solution an objective outsider (not to mention a not-so-objective insider) would consider right or fair. This is a variation on Dad's "difference." The heirs are saying something like: "My *problem* is different."

I've gone through long exploratory discussions with heirs about succession planning in their family businesses, only to find out the answer they are seeking involves some form of financial assassination of other family members.

Succession planning is fine as far as it goes, they admit, but theirs is a different situation. I don't understand how much the success of the company is due to their efforts alone, and what a drain their brothers — or sisters are. . . . And on it goes.

Dad, of course, sees the bubbles rising out of this silent

underwater war, and it bothers him greatly. If they can't get along now, what happen's after I'm gone? See, he protests, my business *is* different. Look at the attitudes my children have. How can anybody else's solution work with this family?

THE 4 PILLARS OF ESTATE PLANNING

As the old saw goes, if you don't know where you're going, any road will take you there. Sure, most family companies have some sort of plan for the estate and the future. It's hard to avoid totally. But it's not enough to have a few technical devices in place. Too often, those "answers" have been pasted together over time to solve immediate problems, or are watered down compromises that don't really benefit anybody. Too often, what little is done (fortunate as it might be) is done without thought to the *many* variables involved, chasing only one or two independent and unrelated goals. These are critical deficiencies.

Planning ownership and management transition in a family company isn't a matter of blinding technical legerdemain, or even Machiavellian politics. It's a process or coordinating interests and objectives. The greatest concerns are concentrated in two major areas: ownership/control and tax avoidance, the latter often absorbing the most energy — and causing the most plans to go awry.

The goal of family business estate planning is most often *continuity,* not the saving of taxes nor even the manipulation of power. While the purity of motives might change as future generations get involved with the business, continuity is usually the goal of the founder as he does his crystal ball gazing at his dependents. Since his plan usually sets the tone for the future, the quality of that initial plan has a lot to do with what future generations do.

There are four pillars supporting every good estate plan, and they each have to carry their part of the weight. If any one is missing or inadequate, or over-built, the plan is almost guaranteed to be unstable, unliveable, and short-lived.

1) Management Transition.

The plan must take survival of the business into account.

To be successful, a family company must have a constant supply of capable, committed, knowledgeable managers. Somehow, provision for management succession has to be considered as an intimate part of the process of deciding where ownership and control are going to be placed. Who will the key managers be after the founder retires or dies? When will this passing of the baton take place and how will it be done?

A realistic look has to be taken at the abilities of the potential family successors (if there are any family successors), and those abilities should be compared to the abilities of the key non-family managers. Are non-family employees, the ones in place today, appropriate for the future? Will new managers be needed? How can they be attracted? What role, if any, will the estate plan have in providing incentive?

2) Placement of Equity Growth.

Ownership and management has to be transferred in a way that minimizes the potential for conflict among future generations. A glance at the problems facing Bill and his family in their welding supply business (see above) presents a fairly distressing picture of what can happen when equity stock is distributed without forethought.

The problem of equity distribution is a most agonizing one for the business owner, who typically has long seen his business as a legacy for his children. A legacy is something one should be able to draw benefit from forever, he thinks quite naturally, so he concludes his heirs should have the benefits of his business forever. He thereby confuses ownership with benefit — a confusion most non-involved minority shareholders are disabused of very early.

In Bill's company, for example, the major conflict between the owning families is a disagreement whether to pay dividends or reinvest for expansion. One option tends to preclude the other.

Quite naturally, Bill would like to see expansion. That solidifies his place in the company — and, besides, he's already taking his "dividends" out in the form of salary. But the stability of those benefits is very fragile for him, because he has no control over the business. The operational rug can be yanked at any time.

His non-involved shareholder/relatives don't have a salary and very few perquisites. They own a significant portion of a sizeable company, yet, for them, there is no "benefit" at all — unless large dividends are paid, something that would turn the company into a cash (and dying?) cow.

Is this the kind of legacy Great Grandad really had in mind for his heirs?

It's important to distinguish carefully between wealth and opportunity in estate planning. Wealth *is* opportunity, but it's an undefined opportunity without a base. Opportunity, of the kind represented by the business, carries the promise of a fairly unlimited future at the price of a relatively limited present. This isn't to say that wealth and opportunity should be distributed independently, but it does imply more variability and richness of options available to The Boss when he makes his plan. He doesn't have to leave opportunity to everybody. In fact, he should leave it only to those who want and can make use of it.

What all this boils down to is two questions:

a) *Should non-working family members share in the equity growth spurred by the work and talent of the family managers?* In most cases, especially where continuity rather than sale of the business is really the major goal, they shouldn't. This approach can remove any incentive for the family managers to manage for growth.

b) *Should working family members be in a position to take salaries and perks while non-involved shareholders receive only paper growth?* Is this really equality of ownership and opportunity?

To take care of both of the above questions, the owner manager is going to have to answer some difficult questions, particularly one that's perhaps the most difficult of all:

➤   *Should the family and the business remain together?* The answer isn't automatically "yes".

3) Assuring Estate Liquidity.

This problem is simple to understand, but often complex

in the solving. There must be a provision made, somehow, to provide enough cash to pay the taxes that are going to be due on the owner's estate. These taxes are definable in advance, so the problem isn't surprise. The problem, instead, is that the family company is almost by nature an illiquid investment — it isn't a quick source of cash. That source has to be planned out in advance, the farther in advance the better.

Here is one of the many areas in which the business owner needs competent professional advice. Someone (most likely an accountant, a banker, or experts in insurance and valuation) has to put together realistic estimates of estate taxes and death costs, but that's only half the job. Once the cash needs are determined, Dad, with professional guidance, has to decide where and how that cash will be found when needed — a highly technical and complex question requiring a great deal of expertise.

4) Minimizing Estate, Income, and Gift Taxes.

Our tax laws are a confused and confusing minefield for any amateur trying to find his way through them, but their very complexity lends a lot of flexibility to the actual planning process. There are many ways to minimize taxes. Professional tax experts have exciting dreams about these things. But none of this help is going to help if the business owner doesn't *ask* for it.

Too often, owner-managers try to answer the questions themselves. Or they ask about a "good book" on the subject:

"Somebody mentioned something about a 303 Redeemer. Where can I find out about that?"

There are a lot of ways to minimize the taxable value of the business, or to set up gifting programs, or to transfer equity growth during the owner's life. But these are complex solutions and they require experts.

The business owner doesn't have to be a tax expert to plan his estate, but he does have to have wisdom and he does have to make the ultimate decisions. Nobody can sign the plan for him. His responsibility is to keep the big picture in mind at all times, to juggle all the conflicting goals, to see the differences and similarities among his heirs.

His job is to ensure that the business survives. If you think that requires the wisdom of Solomon, you're right, but the business owner has an advantage over Solomon. All the important questions have been asked — and answered — somewhere before by other family companies. The Boss doesn't have to decide alone.

DIFFERENT CONSIDERATIONS IN THE THIRD GENERATION

What the founder decides has an impact on the entire future of the business. His considerations, therefore, have to include more than just the next generation — his children and/or his successors. Some thought has to be given to the subsequent generations, because they represent a quantum change from the first and second generations.

These changes are important, because they reflect potential differences in outlook, goals, personal standards, and lifestyle — differences which will all have an impact on the shareholders' relationship to their family's business. Consider some of the more obvious differences between third-generation heirs and their predecessors:

1) Shareholders vary greatly in personal goals, lifestyles, and values.

Many of these differences exist between founders and among brothers and sisters in the first and second generations, but in the third and subsequent generations, the heirs are *cousins* (or even more distant in relationship).

Commonality of experience and culture tends to get thinner and thinner as new generations arise. These individual differences don't necessarily make up a weakness or a problem, not in essence. In fact, it's this sort of diversity that adds strength and vitality to a family. But the lack of a significant shared experience brings with it an increased tendency to misunderstand and disagree.

2) Misunderstandings and disagreements among the shareholders are much more difficult to handle.

While, in most cases, third generation shareholder disagreements aren't necessarily more sticky than disagreements in the first or second generations, there *are* a lot more of them. This simple fact of life, in effect, makes consensus relatively difficult to achieve from the inside. The founder should consider, in his plan, the increasing need for outside influence in maintaining agreement among his heirs.

3) Relatively few shareholders have the desire to become managers of the company.

This is typical among third (and subsequent) generation heirs, and for reasons that should be obvious. With expanding ownership, there is an expanding emotional gap between the business and the potential heirs. The family company is no longer so immediate as a factor in the heir's future, and, in fact, limitations of company size or management requirements can make it fairly obvious that not all heirs can be accommodated. In short, working in the family company is no longer the given career route for all heirs. Thus, estate and management transition planning has to take into account the increasing possibility of non-involved shareholders within subsequent generations.

4) There is a decreasing likelihood that all shareholders will agree with the family "philosophy."

This philosophy is the mission statement, the company motto, the basic commitment to, say, excellence, or quality, or customer service that served the first two generations as the company hallmark. This is the corporate "culture," and as the number of shareholders increase and become more distant from each other, it can no longer be taken for granted that they'll see the company in that single, unified way.

Instead of feeling a commitment to quality, for example, some shareholders might feel that volume and low cost are the keys to profit in a maturing industry. Private branding might be more acceptable to some third-generation shareholders, while it was likely to have been anathema to their predecessors.

There's nothing inherently right about a given "culture," but the founder makes a mistake when he assumes it will (or even should) be shared by all future generations and plans on that assumption.

5) There will probably be less agreement that the business should stay under family ownership.

The founder almost guarantees this sort of disagreement by setting up a cadre of minority, non-involved shareholders through his estate. As has been explained at length elsewhere in this book, minority ownership without management involvement is a snare and an illusion. It's sure not what it's cracked up to be, and third generation non-involved shareholders tend to be a major source of rumblings about sale or merger, particularly in companies that pay only token dividends.

6) There will usually be increasing concern and doubt about the competence of top and middle management.

This is less a reflection on the competence of.the management team than it is a symptom of the existence of non-involved shareholders and their distance from the company. They don't work with the managers. They don't see what is being done. And what they don't know they will misunderstand — and eventually mistrust.

The sooner the founder sets up a clear direction for the company, and a defined qualification process for management, the sooner will this bomb be defused. He cannot, in short, assume the family will always trust management on the premise that management is always going to be the family.

7) Third-generation shareholders are more likely to feel uninformed about company activities and decisions.

And naturally so, in most cases. The farther shareholders are from active management of the company, the more alienated and doubtful they tend to feel. The founder, in his planning, will have to consider this disrupting effect of minority or non-involved ownership. If such shareholders must exist, then a mechanism whereby they can be both informed and have an effect on company direction consistent with their shareholding interest has to be put in place.

The Boss, in short, can't be content to plan the transition only to the second-generation managers. He — and his advisers

— also have to give thought to how the immediate succession plan will effect the third generation heirs. Presumably, The Boss is planning for continuity, not only tax savings or short-term emotional truce. This is a large responsibility.

The question before every business founder is how to go about assuring that his company will continue to grow and prosper as a successful family-owned business. For that to happen, his goal for the future has to be achieving and maintaining fundamental consensus among the shareholders of today and tomorrow.

The key to assuring smooth functioning of the various businesses and investments represented by the family company is the existence of an agreement among the shareholders as to the kind of performance they would like to see from their investment. This isn't to say that we can ever expect complete *agreement* among them — intelligent, capable people inevitably have independent and unique personalities — but there must be a clear and united goal that can be transmitted to management. Achieving this agreement on an ordered and continuing basis is a fundamental factor in successful estate planning.

Achieving this clarity requires more than a few shareholder meetings. It requires a fundamental understanding of the situation the company will find itself in with the advent of the third generation of owners. This understanding is a key, both to understanding the problems and deciding on roads to solution.

Typically, in a company with second-generation management (usually run by brothers, but, obviously, variations are possible), the management style is relatively informal and collaborative. Each second-generation manager finds his or her own strengths and abilities, and directs management activities in those directions. This break from the entrepreneurial style represented by the founder is usually difficult, but in the companies that survive, that break was usually made.

But consider the problems and new challenges that arise with the arrival of the third generation:

1) Heirs have greater freedom in career choice.

It is at least an equal chance that third-generation heirs

will decide on career options outside the family company. This raises complications because it usually requires the recruitment and development of non-family key managers, and because it sets up a potential conflict between the managing and non-managing cousins and siblings.

2) Decision about successor management goes from the hands of a very few (founder or founders), into the hands of a widening "bureaucracy."

The potential successor CEO — family or non-family — has many rather than few people to please, and usually finds very little agreement or consensus among that crowd as to precisely what constitutes the qualifying attributes.

3) Income ceases to be a major issue for the owners, yielding instead to concerns about asset management and tax planning.

If a company has survived through the second generation of management (and assuming it survived in good health), a state of affluence exists which changes the perspective from which the owners do their planning — and disagreeing. Difficult as relative compensation issues can be, shareholders are much more interdependent (and, therefore, confined) on issues of communal asset management.

4) Concerns for getting things going and making things work yield to concerns for keeping things going.

This new problem, by definition, requires institutionalization of policies, planning, and management qualification. The "old days" where a good tinkerer or a brilliant trouble shooter could save the day fade to pleasant memories. This new concern brings with it, too, some previously "unthinkable" options which must be considered in planning continuity. Essentially, four possibilities are open to the third-generation family company, and the decision among them must be made consciously, with full consideration of the factors important to their desirability:

a) Remain Family-Owned: Is it important to maintain family privacy and management? Are there enough family managers available to make this possible and necessary? Can non-family professional management be sufficiently motivated under these conditions (particularly if the pool of family managers is low or empty)? Is the attendant limitation on financial resources acceptable?

b) Go Public: Is the family willing to give up privacy? Will it be possible to maintain control and family management? Is this maintenance of control desirable? Will the positive impact of the capital infusion justify the tradeoffs? Is going public possible?

c) Merge with a Larger Company: Is the family willing to give up control for the sake of investment liquidity? Would this be the only source of the required management talent and financial resources for significant growth (and, therefore, return on investment)?

d) Sell: Should the family sell outright and leave to others the risks and rewards the company represents? Are shareholder disagreements so intense and involved that further leadership or direction are impossible? Are there no possible family managers, now or in the future? Is the future of the company in doubt?

Some of these options would have been blasphemy to the founder and, often, to this successors. With the passage of time, however, their existence as options increasingly demands recognition and consideration.

5) The owners become more emotionally distant.

In most any family, the emotional closeness among cousins tends to have an inverse relation to the passage of time. The fact that these cousins might share ownership in a successful company doesn't seem to have a lot of impact on changing this differentiation. This isn't to say that the wider family disintegrates or dissipates. It simply becomes less focused than it was in the preceding generation.

In the typical family, this isn't mourned (except maybe by the older folks who remember the family holiday gatherings which are long passed), but in a family that owns a business, it generates an increasing white noise of conflicting signals to the management of the company — not to mention an increasing sensitivity in family business discussions.

6) The CEO of a third-generation company can be truly effective only under one of two circumstances:

a) He is able to function as a powerful, respected "head of the clan," or

b) He is able to operate under a charter given to him by the family in the form of shared family goals.

Disappearing forever in the third-generation company is the day of the self-defined patriarch (or matriarch). Clearly, the possibility of such a "charter," or, as an alternative, the existence of such a tribal leader will have a great impact on decisions made with regard to the issues raised above.

WHY OUTSIDE REVIEW IS ESSENTIAL

The above aren't the only questions facing a family business in transition. There are always business, market, product, and financial decisions to be made. But the above succession and continuity issues necessarily emerge as the most fundamental concerns of estate planning. They emerge out of the natural course of events, out of the company's passage through its lifecycle, out of the dilution of ownership control, and out of the increasing diversity among the shareholders.

The statement that these problems exist is in no way symbolic of a value judgment on the shareholders or the company. Their existence is as natural as is the dubious joy of puberty for an adolescent. The trick is to survive the process intact so that the benefits of the attendant changes can be enjoyed.

Estate planning raises a lot of technical questions. Competent technical help will be required, to be sure. There are many financial, legal, tax, and organizational issues to be addressed. But even capable technical advisers will find it difficult to operate without an objective interface between them and the ownership of the company. Competent management will be required, too, but even the most professional manager will find it impossible to achieve opposing goals or to satisfy a range of disagreeing superiors.

Management, too, needs an interface between them and the owners. This need may or may not be intense between the successor(s) and the founder, but will almost surely be a major factor for the successors' heirs.

The third-generation shareholders will most likely need an interface between themselves and the company, someone to act as a filter for ideas, an arbitrator of valid disagreements, a catalyst for consensus, and a translator of that consensus into planning and management action.

The founder should assume there will almost always be some disagreement among shareholders, particularly among third and subsequent generation owners. This eventuality should be assumed, accepted, and worked with. Decisions about the future should be made with those differing goals and attitudes placed in the balance.

His goal in planning — his primary goal, given more importance than tax savings or immediate "fairness" — should be encouraging and maintaining a necessary shareholder consensus — the desire to do what's best for the company.

An excellent, proven, and effective repository for the responsibility of maintaining this consensus can be a working board of objective, committed and trusted outsiders — the subject of the next and final chapter.

Chapter 9
SEEKING — AND ACCEPTING — OUTSIDE REVIEW
"But My Business Is DIFFERENT"

> *The easiest thing of all is to deceive one's self; for what a man wishes, he generally believes to be true.*
>
> **Demosthenes**

Most family businesses operate on a managerial flood plain. They didn't locate there on purpose. The river just sort of finds them, wherever they are.

At first nobody notices the change in terrain, because the managers are just too busy and confused to notice much of anything. But the blithe ignorance is only temporary. Inevitably, the river of trouble makes itself known. Suddenly, usually late one exhausting night, family managers awake in the midst of a flood, adrift in a wash of problems, frantically treading water, wondering where the river came from — not to mention how it managed to get so high.

And, after that first recognition, the problems never seem to recede.

This is the way it is. For most family companies, trouble is a creeping, seeping thing — not a sudden catastrophe. Flash floods they could handle, because most family managers are used to handling the unexpected gullywashers. They're masters at sandbagging. Instead, what gets them is the slow drizzle, the gradually rising tide.

Almost without notice the days get longer, family managers start working at night, at home, and on weekends. As the rising flood approaches their sensitive parts, the family managers respond in the only way they know. They just swim harder and longer as the disasters multiply and diversify. Brush fires, lightning strikes, earthquakes, and avalanches occur one after another. Each draws full attention and energy — at least until the next crisis, when the old one is necessarily dropped, unfinished and unresolved.

Everybody looks forward, wistfully, to "when things settle down" and they can get straightened out. But, somehow, the company never seems to run out of new market concerns, territories, people needs, personnel problems, competitive disasters — you name it. And, there are never enough people.

No wonder family business managers fall behind. And no wonder they don't have time, or energy, or even the inclination to think about the future in any organized way. Dad's working like a coal mine mule and the successors are busily learning the same ropes. What other model do they have?

All of this work is visually very impressive — lots of smoke and dust and flailing about — but no matter how stunning the sight, one fact doesn't change: managers under constant distraction and exhaustion don't manage very well at all.

What has all this to do with outside review? If family business managers are all that buried, the last thing they would seem to need is another variable in their already over-stocked equation.

Well, the answer hinges around the question of effectiveness. A lot of experience on the part of a lot of family companies has proven over and over again that, left to itself, the family business finds it almost impossible to break the descending spiral of work leading to more work leading to more work, with less and less getting done.

There's nothing inherent in hard work to guarantee effectiveness, and even if there were a guarantee, there's usually no real way to measure it. What's the standard, after all? There's Dad's measure, of course, but his standard is sweat, which is input rather than outcome: "We just aren't working hard enough." As far as he's concerned, there's no *time* for "measurement." There's too much to do.

His successors aren't in much better shape. By the time the flood overflows the banks, most of the early bloom is off the family business career rose. They can't seem to get Dad's respect, his direct commitment to management transition, or any information on his plans for them (if, indeed, he has any). The business seems buried, disorganized. It's management by flap. In all the dust and noise, their ideas are ignored (which, to add to the dust and confusion, means their spouses are losing faith in the possibility of it all working out).

The mighty family business engine is racing. The tach is almost redlined. The doors are locked. The tinted windows are up. Everybody's anxious, waiting to go somewhere, but nobody knows quite how to get the family business in gear.

If only we could just *ask* somebody . . .

WHY THE BOSS WON'T ASK FOR HELP

Thus comes the first inkling that maybe some sort of outside help would be good. But, wait a minute. Remember that one of the great advantages of owning one's own business is privacy. By staying our own boss, we can make sure nobody knows "nuttin," and it's relatively easy to keep it that way as completely and as long as possible.

This is a Good Thing, right?

In some ways, yes. It depends on one's point of view. If privacy in and of itself is the major objective, then the absence of "nosey," "pushy" examiners *would* be a Good Thing. On the other hand, if continuity, succession, growth, and profitability are the major goals — as we've assumed all along they are — lack of outside review is everything *but* a Good Thing. It's an open invitation to a corporate drowning.

If the family business is going to succeed, generation to generation, someone is going to have to teach the managers to swim — and maybe help a little with flood control.

Trouble is, too many family companies are "closed" corporations in fact as much as in legal terminology. Few have any kind of outside review of management judgments, decisions, and policies. Far too few have available to them any expertise, knowledge, or advice other than what they get from insiders — the same insiders who've been drawing on the same data base over and over again for almost a generation.

This doesn't happen because they can't afford outside help. It happens because the insiders like things that way. The very thought of having some outsider poking around in the business tends to make the family manager's every bodily aperture pucker up with revulsion.

"We didn't spend all this energy building our own business," they say, righteously, "just so somebody else can second-guess our judgments."

This doesn't mean they don't ask for input to their decisions. They do — but only from very carefully selected, fundamentally "safe" sources.

Who are these "sources"? Well, The Boss, of course. He runs the show very well, thank you, and makes sure everybody knows it. But who else? A few key inside managers, maybe, as well as the oldest son — with some severe limits. If Dad has a trusted adviser (attorney, banker, etc.), he might run a few ideas by him. But The Boss makes all the *real* decisions by himself. Remember, that's the only person he's really learned to trust.

At least The Boss has his professional advisers, you're probably thinking — his attorney, accountant, banker, insurance underwriter, and so forth. At least they're around to keep him out of trouble.

So we would hope — but this isn't any more likely than his having a real board. In the first place, Dad doesn't have a lot of respect for professional advisers. (After all, if they're so smart, why aren't they making the kind of money he is?) In the second place, their fee meters are always running, and much too fast. Because of the fees they charge, The Boss isn't about to use them for casual advice or informal brainstorming (unless, of course, he's managed to get them on his board and working for expenses, plus lunch).

The advisers, on their part, don't help matters much, either. They go along with Old Dad, passively accepting the fact that he doesn't use them as he should. "He's just that way. He's stubborn. He's tough. He's not about to listen to anybody."

"We can recommend," they tend to say in understandable rationalization, "but it's up to him to accept our advice. We can't force him."

The result of this tendency by The Boss and his advisers to rationalize can be seen in the dusty, unsigned estate plan, the inadequate accounting system, the poorly administered pension fund, the confused insurance setup, and the lack of sophisticated cash management and financing.

The Boss, you see, does all these things himself. His business is "different." He's going to get around to his estate plan, even has some thoughts on it, but economic conditions are forcing him to spend all of his waking hours making the buck.

His accounting system was "carefully evolved" to fit his unique situation ("My business is different"). He's not about to let some *banker* manage his money ("He never made a buck in his life"), and insurance is a game that agents play with him to raise their commissions ("I always buy term").

The Boss is used to being good at what he does. He quite easily confuses talent with ability and success with omnipotence. If he did it so well in truck fenders, uniform rental, or wholesale parts, then who better to do just as well in estate planning, accounting, finance, and management in general? All he really needs is a little more time — maybe when The Kid has more of a handle on things and Dad can spend more time on policy decisions. Know any good books?

Of course, The Kid never really gets a handle on things and Old Dad never really finds the time to handle all of these policy matters.

But don't worry. He will. He will. When the river crests.

At least The Boss has his board of directors to go to. Right?

Half right, maybe. He does *have* a board. Because of the nature of our tax laws, most successful family companies find it's worth their while to incorporate. This, naturally, means that most successful family companies have boards of directors.

But that's usually about all it means.

In actuality, family business boards — and the "directors" who make them up — have about as much reality and substance as a politician's promise. Because of this (assuming 95+ % of our corporations are closely held), most of the corporate directors in this country are unqualified to hold their positions.

The reason so many corporations survive despite their unqualified directors is the reality (and for this we should be grateful) that those directors have no real responsibilities. They can't do any active harm because they're mostly inactive. This is only a negative safety, though. In the long term, they produce a vacuum that sucks up much of the potential of the companies they "direct."

Most family business boards are shams. It's a fact of life. They're products of amateur playwrights. The board meetings are held in The Boss's imagination or, at best, in the hallway as The Boss and his henchmen hatch their plots on the run — and the attorney carefully composes the "minutes" out of his word processing files.

In general, the business owner does the directing, the other directors (Mom, The Kid, The Grateful Employee, The Retired Old Buddy) serve as the "directees" and sign on whatever dotted line The Boss points to — while the attorney gives it all a patina of respectability.

Most board meetings "held" in this country are never held at all.

THE BEST HELP — OUTSIDE REVIEW

If The Boss and the successors wanted just one technique, one sure-cure miracle "drug" that could solve their problems, the closest they could come is the elimination of their profound isolation. Far too many family companies are fortresses with rusted chains and jammed drawbridges. Sure, entrepreneurship is a solitary occupation — but it doesn't have to be lonely. Solitude means freedom and creativity. Loneliness is just plain bad business.

But who could make it "unlonely"?

Well, bear with me for another paragraph or two. Just for the sake of discussion, let's create a fictional person. Let's create someone who is successful, at a crest in his or her career. Let's make this person intelligent, articulate, and widely experienced. Assume, too, that this person has a lot of business experience, most of it running his or her successful company. This person has been farther than we have, done more things, made more mistakes, and learned more lessons. This person also knows us and respects our needs and goals. Most of all, this person wants to help, for the sole reason that he or she enjoys wrestling with business problems. He or she has no personal interest in the direction our decisions take, only in their reasonability and quality.

Who is this person, and why did I create him or her?

I'll be blunt. This person is the ideal outside director for a family company — yours, mine, the other guy's.

We already know about the standard board in the typical family company. It's a nonentity, dedicated to the service of The Boss's inclinations. But, by bringing up this whole issue of "outside review," I'm essentially suggesting that most successful family businesses would solve a great part of their problems by creating a *real, working board of outside directors,* a board consisting of a *majority* of outside directors such as the person described above.

This idea gets a varied response from the people I talk to. Successors are usually *very* interested, not always for the best reasons. Hey, they say, that ain't a bad idea. It would be a good way to control the Old Man. Dad's reaction, on the other hand, is often something on the order of "LIKE HELL!"

He says: "You give me a reason, one good reason, why

I should put in a bunch of smart alecks, sit them down on my Board, and after they've looked around the business, studied the operation, and determined where we've been and where we're going — they come for the first board meeting and tell me, 'Charlie, we're glad you asked us to serve on your board. We've looked at your business, and we've determined what the problem is. It's YOU. You're fired.'

"Now why would I want to expose myself to something like that?" Charlie will ask me.

"Charlie," I'll tell him, "all you've got to do is say 'Thank you, gentlemen,' walk out in the hall, hold a shareholders' meeting, and have the following conversation with yourself:

" 'Well, Shareholders, what do you think about this board?'

"And the Shareholder says: 'I don't know Charlie. I don't think they're competent.'

"So Charlie responds: 'Okay, let's dismiss them.'

"With this decided, Charlie," I say to him, "There's only one more item of business:

" 'Oh, by the way, Charlie,' the shareholders tell you as you walk back in to fire the directors, 'you're rehired.' "

The fact is, Dad doesn't give away any formal power by creating an outside board. Instead, he's opening up the business to his own powers by asking for help from the very people who can best give him the help he needs.

All the bluster Dad puts up is a smoke screen. This great American hero who's at the top of his career, at the pinnacle of his climb, in the presidency of his trade association, is, behind his private, closed doors scared half to death, confused, and watching his time run out steadily, inexorably. But few people, other than Dad, himself, Mom, and the successors (if they're unusually sensitive) know the truth about this entrepreneurial behemoth.

All of his secrecy, all of the habits he's built into his style, all of the peculiar structures he's put into his business, have boxed him into an almost inescapable position. He can't talk to Mom, because she'll worry. He can't talk to the kids because they don't understand. He can't talk to the employees because they'll get the wrong idea. He can't talk to anybody, not even his advisers, because they aren't any good. They're all "bums."

Maybe you're right, Dad will admit, reluctantly, but why do you want me to fool around with my board? The only reason I have one is because I have to. They do what I want them to do. I have my board and the little old "Dragon" keeping my books who thinks just like me. Leave me that, at least.

Okay. You've got it. Now what do you do? Don't ask anybody, Boss. Figure it out yourself.

What I'm suggesting — and I'm fully aware that this is probably the hardest thing anybody could ask a business owner to do — is to take a long, honest look at himself and his business. Do this early in the morning, before coffee, if possible. Look in the mirror and say a couple of times in succession:

"You know something? I need Help. I really do need help. This business needs help. My successors need help. My employees, God help them, need help. Do they know this company is going to continue forever? Do I know it? It's all on my shoulders. I don't want to handle it alone anymore. I'm starting to lose control. There are too many things happening. I don't know what to do."

Sure, that's a lot to say into a mirror before coffee. But just the act of saying it is a major breakthrough. Assuming the exercise is carried on over a period of a few months, Dad is likely to begin thinking about a real board without developing psychological carbuncles. He may even make up his mind and decide to go out and actually form himself a board.

WHY "REAL" BOARDS AREN'T "WORKING" BOARDS

But we're not out of the swamp yet. We have to take a look at the kind of board Dad's likely to put together. Here's a little sample of his reasoning:

"Let's see. There's my friend, Bruce. He's been a buddy of mine for years. He'll understand. I'll put Bruce on the board. And there's also my key man, my director of purchasing who's been with me for 30 years. He and I are reaching 65 together.

I'll put him on the board, too. Now, who else? Well, there's my lawyer, of course. I'll just keep him on the board. And then there's my brother who has 25% of the business. I don't know why I did that, but I did, so I'll put him on the board to keep him quiet.

"How about The Kid? Yeah, that's a good idea. He won't say much, but that's okay. Then there's my retired friend, Lefkowitz. He's got nothing to do, just sits around all day, bored. He'll be grateful as hell, so I'll ask him, too."

Dad has decided to put together an outside board, but what he's really created is a board of grateful employees, miserable successors, antiquated ex-managers, henchmen, and compatriots all of whom are guaranteed to agree with everything he says on all the really important issues. It's a brilliant stratagem — one that's guaranteed to keep him comfortable and looking good.

It's a nice try, and even with its flaws often better than nothing, but this isn't the sort of board The Boss, the business, and everybody else really needs. These people aren't really going to do what's needed. What The Boss needs is somebody really able to help.

Who can help? Well, definitely not (repeat: NOT) relatives. If Dad wants the advice of his relatives he doesn't really have to ask. They'll just keep right on volunteering. Successors and heirs won't be much help, either. After all, Dad's never listened to what they had to say in the past, and, besides, they're the people the board will be judging for future responsibility in the business. How can they be asked to judge themselves?

What about employees? Well, the best way to become an ex-employee is to take a position as The Boss's director seriously enough to actually disagree with his opinions. Suppliers and customers, too, should be rejected as soon as they're thought of. This should go without saying, but I've seen them sitting on boards.

What about advisers? Well, if we have the attorney or accountant on the board, what do we get from them that we wouldn't get from a phone call or a meeting in their office? Besides, how objective can we ask a non-disinterested human being to be? Can we expect to sit them down at a board meeting and ask them to decide whether or not our law firm is doing the job for us? ("What do you think, Director Sullivan? Is Sullivan, Sullivan, and O'Malley really the best law firm we could get?")

If we need help from our advisers, all we have to do is ask them, and be willing to pay for the answers.

So who's left? Friends? Why would we want to put a friend on the board? Here we take somebody who's been talking to us and helping us for years and ask him suddenly to become a formal adviser. What kind of position does that put a friend in? Best to let the friend speak for himself: "I love you, Charlie. Don't make me a director, because I might have to disagree with you — I mean really disagree on something really important. I don't want to be in that position. I love you too much. We're good friends. If you want my help, I'll give it to you, as a friend, but don't put that kind of pressure on me."

We really don't want good friends as directors.

That's great, you're thinking. You just wiped out everyone I know. Who's left, anyway?

Well, remember who it is we're supposed to be looking for as an outside director. This is a person who can help make sure our business continues as long and as successfully as possible. It's someone who can help with growth, with transition planning, with the selection and qualification of successors. We're looking for someone to help us do all the things we need to do for the future, to help carry out the transition plan that's been the subject of this book.

Who better to do that than someone who understands the whole process of running a business and taking the risks? Who better than someone who has struggled with succession problems — and successors? Who better to do this than other business owners, and men and women used to managing risk?

What The Boss needs is someone who can understand without looking down (or up) their noses, someone who can have consideration and compassion for the problems that come with business ownership. The Boss needs someone who can say, "By God, Charlie, I went through the same thing myself. Here's what

I did to solve it." The Boss needs someone he can look in the eye and whose suggestions he will actually listen to and act upon.

A WORKING BOARD — WHEN?

While every family company needs some form of outside review, not every family company needs a working board of outside directors. It just isn't appropriate in some cases. In others, a working board would be a real distraction from the business at hand.

But, wait. Before you go away, relieved, ask yourself — and answer — the following questions. A "no" answer to any one of them will let you off the hook. If you answer each in the affirmative, gird your loins and start going through your list of risk-taking peers. You're ready for a real board.

Question 1: Is my company successful?

Is your company an established, going concern? Do you — and your employees, customers, suppliers, and creditors — have reason to believe your company is likely to be around in the future?

A real board couldn't really add a lot to a new venture. That's the job of the entrepreneur, probably best accomplished in the solitude of his own dream and his own sweat. Outside directors would just clutter up his decision making. Nor would a real board be very helpful at damage control or emergency surgery on a company in deep trouble. The board doesn't have the tools, the energy, the consistent involvement required for accomplishing a turnaround.

But once a company has survived the horrendous early years and once the problems have been brought to heel at a manageable level, the time has come to look beyond the present to how the business can be kept successful next year and in the next decade. Because this kind of thinking is easily cluttered by present concerns, it's the kind of thinking for which a board is admirably suited.

Question 2: Is my management team structured and reasonably stable?

If things are run by Mom and Pop, or Dad, the Kids, and a few manual laborers, there's not a lot of company to direct. Ownership and management under these conditions are one and the same thing and nobody has the inclination, the time, or the job description to allow for much planning. A real board could direct all it wanted, and very little would be likely to happen.

But by the time success has become a fact for a family company, that company should be getting used to dealing with both ownership and management questions — and knowing the difference between each. Success brings with it the requirement to begin separating the concerns of ownership from the concerns of management before they become hopelessly and disastrously confounded with each other. The separation is possible — in philosophy if not in fact. It involves setting up viable measures of performance, thinking beyond the present quarter, defining responsibilities, compensation, and management structure.

Directors need "directees." They need to know whom to talk to about what. They need to have standards for judging performance and there must be compensation systems to set or change. A board needs a real organization within which to get things done.

If you look into your company and find the "lightning rod" form of organization (The Boss, The Help, and no insulation in between) or a "wagon wheel" (The Boss at the hub, each employee isolated at the end of a "spoke"), two things need to happen before you're ready for a real board:

1) *Understand that your organization is congruent with the organizations of far more family companies than you realize — so your company isn't all that different.*

2) *Do something about setting up a middle management. Delegate, promote, reorganize, define, do whatever is necessary to lighten the burden carried by The Boss and get more brains into the decision-making system.*

Once all this is done, or at least in process, the prospective board will have something to direct.

Question 3: Are my managers and advisers competent?

This question isn't as easy to answer as it might seem. The competence referred to here is competence at managing change and preparing for the future. While ability to manage or advise the present business is useful and necessary, a growing business has problems of the future. A real board will point management to that future and expect them to respond. If they're not ready or able to do so, the board's input will be wasted.

What good is a conductor if the members of the orchestra can't read the music he gives them?

Depending on your answers, you are either ready for a board or you have some work to do before a board is necessary. In either case, doing nothing is fully and completely inappropriate.

A WORKING BOARD — HOW?

The actual mechanics of creating and using an outside board aren't all that complicated. In fact, the highest hurdle is the "gotta wanna" jump. No board of directors has ever made a difference in any family company unless the owner of that business really, honestly, and openly *wanted* the board's help — and used it.

That's step one of putting a real board together, an honest soul-searching to see if you are, in fact, serious about asking your peers for help and willing to give them enough information to understand the problem. If, *in fact,* your company meets the qualifications listed above and if, *in fact,* you really "wanna" create a board, the hard part is over. Now all you need to do is find the directors you need, court them, convince them, organize them, inform them, meet with them and reap all the benefits.

Those are the relatively easy parts, but still worth going into in some detail.

A WORKING BOARD — WHO?

Given the sort of long-range strategic decisions that will concern a working board of directors, a business owner looking for outsiders to fill seats on that board should look for men or women who can do one, some, or all of the following:

- Expand financial knowledge and skill
- Fill in experience gaps for present management
- Expand on present management strengths
- Help understand and manage business growth
- Advise the owner on the complexities of estate planning
- Bring objectivity and good judgement to the training and selection of successors
- Work together with other outside directors to produce a board much smarter than the sum of its component parts

Not every successful person, even one meeting the qualifications above is right for the board of a successful family-owned business. This is more than a business position. In many ways, it's also a *family* position. Outside directors need to be able to work with all the human and emotional variables that are so important in a family business. Technicians, no matter how brilliant, in the end won't be able to do the job asked of them.

Here are some personal qualities and background characteristics the ideal outside director should have:

- Proven ability which is apparent to any qualified observer
- Holder of significant responsibility
- Familiarity with, and understanding of, the process of risk-taking for profit
- Absolute independence of the business owner and the company
- Courage of opinion
- Ability to look the business owner and the successors in the eye and tell them the truth — with compassion and understanding
- Patience and perseverance

Probably the best summary of all these characteristics is to describe an ideal director as somebody The Boss, the successors, the heirs, the spouses, and everybody else involved can trust and respect.

WHERE TO FIND DIRECTORS

Business owners are shy people. I know that sounds ridiculous, but when it comes to asking for help from high-powered people, the business owner seems always to wind up thinking he's somehow unworthy. He can sell anybody anything, under any conditions, but when it comes to inviting his peers to serve on his board, he wilts into a wallflower more retiring than a prepubescent boy at his first dance.

How can he get over this shyness? Something that helps is to reverse roles, mentally, and consider how it would feel to be *invited* to serve as somebody else's director. Most owner-managers would admit they'd be flattered by the invitation. Most would further admit there's some attraction in the chance to work on somebody else's problems for once, to apply the lessons that seem so difficult to apply to one's own difficulties. This isn't to mention the fascination in learning how another business and/or industry operates, or the real kick one can get out of working with a roomful of really competent people.

Looked at in this light, is it really surprising that most people who are invited to serve as outside directors actually say "yes"? And those who decline, most often do so with regret. No, the problem shouldn't be asking. Once the prospective director is found, the invitation should be the enjoyable part.

But how and where is he or she found? Usually in the same places we find the business owner. Prospective outside directors are all around. The Boss meets them all the time — at the club, at Rotary meetings, on the golf course, on hospital or bank boards. They are usually where he is. He just never noticed them before, never talked *business* with them before. He never really got to know them.

Remember that competent people tend to know each other. There's no reason why you can't just ask around. And picture your reaction if you got a phone call one day and heard: "I was just talking to Bill Smith and he told me you're one of the smartest business owners in town. Could we get together?"

You're going to say no?

The actual courtship is a more leisurely process. It's a blending and testing of personalities, perspectives, and chemistry. There's no need to be aggressive in the beginning, no real need for "Hi, I'm Frank Cohen and I'm lookin' for directors." The acquaintance of capable people alone is enough to justify the time spent together. As for the directorship, if it's right, the time will present itself.

WHAT ARE DIRECTORS PAID?

There are no rules about directors fees — not as to the absolute dollar amounts, that is — but there are some helpful guidelines. Fees paid to family business directors vary in absolute amounts from small, per-meeting honoraria of $250, up to annual fees as high as $20,000 or more.

Directors who meet the qualifications listed above don't *need* high fees as supplements to their income, but they surely do appreciate them — both because money is always useful, and because money is a mutually understood symbol of commitment and worth. If the director knows that the director fee is high enough that the business owner winces when he signs the check, he'll know that business owner is serious about his board. The flip side of this is the business owner's knowledge that a director who accepts this significant fee will feel a responsibility to deliver the help requested.

Absolute dollars aren't so important as the significance of the fees that are paid. Don't weaken the mutual commitment by tying attendance at meetings to payment of fees. Don't think a few bucks, a jug of cheap wine and a deli platter demonstrate your commitment to a real board.

Pay significant fees and expect significant help. Do this, and it's sure to happen.

HOW MANY DIRECTORS, FOR HOW LONG?

Boards should be manageable bodies, filled with people who are fresh and open to new ideas. The "manageable" part can be assured with a board of between five to nine directors (less than five and it's hardly a "body"; more than nine, it tends to become a mob). The fresh and open part can be handled by building into the board a set rotation, say three to four years per director, staggered to maintain continuity.

While insiders are appropriate on the board, their number should be held to a minimum — and under no circumstances should insiders outnumber the outsiders! Most typically, the owner-manager-CEO will serve as chairman. Other insiders on the board might be the company controller, a significant (or equivalent) owner, or a representative of major blocks of stock. There are often pressing reasons to have one or more of these people serve as directors. Nevertheless, the goal should be to construct the board and its communication channels such that a *directorship* is not the only way to make people comfortable with how the business is being managed.

Agitation for insider seats on the board of directors is usually a symptom of communication breakdown, and it most typically comes from minority shareholders who aren't involved in the day-to-day operation of the company. Since a properly designed outside board should be one of the greatest comforts a minority shareholder could have (outside of high dividends or liquidation of stock, of course), their discomfort should be addressed and dealt with.

Shareholders need a real sense of the competence, commitment, and talent of their board. This can be done a number of ways. Shareholders can be invited to meetings periodically (either as a group or as individuals) as observing guests. Watching a good board in operation can be an awe-inspiring thing. For longer-term understanding and involvement, shareholder representatives can take positions as "associate" or "pro tem" directors, with no formal place on the board, but the open invitation to attend all meetings for a significant length of time (at least 18 months).

Two objectives are worth pursuing. First, everybody in the company should be familiar with the board, should feel they know what it is doing (at the level of detail their position rates), and should be convinced of its disinterested objectivity. Secondly, a culture should be built in which everyone desires the maximum number of qualified outsiders on the board (implying, therefore, the minimum number of insiders).

THE QUESTION OF LIABILITY

Directors do have liability. It is something every director and every business owner should realize and deal with. Fortunately, assuming honesty and commitment, in the majority of companies this liability is minimized by the fact that the owner-manager is the only shareholder. Since the major liability would be the possibility of a shareholder suit, and since The Boss, as a director, couldn't very well sue himself, liability in these cases is negligible. Where there are many shareholders, however, and particularly where groups of shareholders are in disagreement, the liability problem becomes more significant.

Where some potential for liability exists, there also exist alternatives for indemnifying directors through insurance or other approaches. Only in the most extreme or unstable companies is the liability question, by itself, enough reason to avoid creating a working, outside board.

POTENTIAL PROBLEMS WITH OUTSIDE DIRECTORS

A working board isn't a panacea. It takes a lot of work to form and a lot more work to run. The commitment it requires is long-term, and boards have highs and lows like any organization.

Outside directors, particularly when a rotation system doesn't exist or is overridden too often can become an entrenched part of the problems rather than managers of solution. Poor agendas and poor meeting management can allow boards to get involved with day-to-day tactical considerations which the directors are not qualified to tackle (e.g. hiring and firing of middle managers, product pricing, and the like).

Directors can inadvertently become embroiled in personal conflicts, and be perceived as standing for one side or the other. Directors can be so poorly informed (or even misinformed) by the operating managers that their decisions and advice are wrong for the company.

All of these problems and more can occur with outside boards, but when such difficulties are placed on a scale opposite the benefits this chapter has outlined, the problems pale in significance. The creation of a working board of outside directors can be the most meaningful and positive step a business owner can take to ensure the continued success and survival of his business. It can be a great help (and an even greater — but presumably welcome — challenge) to the successors. It can also be a great comfort to the successors' spouses.

Most of all, an outside board can serve to break down the heavy walls surrounding the family company. It can lubricate the locks. It can lower the drawbridge.

It can, in short, open the family company to the fresh air and sunshine of the outside world.

Outside review is an essential ingredient in making sure all the "processes" of succession planning are put in place and honestly carried out. Without this kind of help, the family business is too much like a truck with no clutch. The engine is powerful, the drive train is there, ready to move, but there's no mechanism for connecting the two and keeping them connected.

It's a potentially good life, the life in the successful family company. But like paradise, it has to be earned in the face of a lot of powerful and seductive temptations.

Isn't this the time to begin earning what we've all really wanted all along?

INDEX

ALSO AVAILABLE from Business Succession Resource Center and Jamieson Press:

●**"THE BOSS'S DAUGHTER: A Report on America's Fastest Growing Group of Family Business Successors"** by Cindy Ross Hitchcock.

...A tour of life as a business owner's daughter-successor, guided and narrated by the "Bosses' Daughters" themselves. **More than 100 women, of all ages, working in family businesses in many different industries, took part in a two-year study of bosses' daughters,** conducted by Business Succession Resource Center and Cindy Hitchcock, a daughter-successor herself and leading sales producer in her industry.

This is the first book written about this emerging force in family business, with its many exciting possibilities as well as its new and unique set of problems — a story told by those who've lived it. The lessons, the experiences, the warnings, and the advice all come from women who have seen and know what challenges daughter-successors must face — and who've learned how to meet them.

●**THE MICRO-DIRECTOR**tm — Family Business Software for the IBM-PC, designed by Janet L. Halliday. **Technical Adviser:** John Ward, Ph.D., Loyola University.

...A totally unique approach to a new and powerful business tool — the personal computer. **"THE MICRO-DIRECTOR**tm**"** is designed to function as your "outside director," leading you through a real-world strategic analysis of your financial statements and your market position — just as a working director would do. Under **"THE MICRO-DIRECTOR'S**tm**"** guidance, you'll get an entirely new picture of readily available information.

The **"FINANCIAL STATEMENT ANALYST"** helps key family managers read and analyze financial statements for important trends and strategic information. The **"MARKET SHARE ANALYST"** helps family and non-family managers estimate what's happening to the company's market share — a key element of growth and profitability. Both programs produce full color graphic pictures and visual comparisons for your management and planning use. An exciting new tool to help families in business work **together** to analyze the business and plan for the future.

— Requires IBM-PC, 128K, two disc drives, color graphics board. (Matrix printer optional, but recommended.)

**Jamieson
Press**
Post Office Box 909
Cleveland, Ohio 44120
216/752-7970